Chongqing
Tourist Guide

Compiled by the Chongqing
Tourism Bureau

China Travel & Tourism Press

Editors-in-Chief:	Wang Qingyu	Li Renzhi	
Deputy Editors-in-Chief:	Zou Jiping	Sun Yimin	Wu Huailian
	Han Yuhui	Huang Jinshan	Zhang Runsheng
Editorial Board:	Wang Qingyu	Li Renzhi	Huang Jinshan
	Zhang Runsheng	Zhang Hong	Zou Jiping
	Sun Yimin	Wu Huailian	Han Yuhui
	Xiao Chuan		
Text by	Ran Zhuang	Sun Shanqi	Lu Daqian
Translated by	Gao Fan		
Managing Editor:	Lu Daqian		
Designed by	Daqian Studio		

Photographers (in the order of the number of strokes of surnames):

Yu Bin	Wan Hong	Bian Chong
Wan Benliang	Wang Qingyu	Wang Jinghua
Zheng Yunfeng	Deng Qingyun	Deng Hui
Liu Wangyang	Bai Zhiyong	Bai Hai
Tian Jiemin	Lu Daqian	Qi Baogui
Ren Zhenxue	Qiao Debing	Zhu Yilin
Zhu Jian	Jiang Bingxi	Li Wenqiao
Li Yongzhong	Li Kai	Li Xia
Li Bin	He Zhihong	He Liangshu
Song Mingkun	Wu Shengyan	Wu Xiaoming
Xiao Chuan	Gu Weiheng	Zhang Shuren
Zhang Zuoliang	Zhang Chushu	Zhang Yuyang
A Bing	Luo Dawan	Luo Xianfeng
Lu Gang	Yang Shaoquan	Yang Shuping
Chen Jun	Chen Daocheng	Chen Chichun
Chen Jian	Jin Yuxi	Meng Xuezhen
Zhao Guilin	Fei Ning	Hu Weiguo
Qin Daizuo	E Yi	Gao Jianshe
Geng Xu	Xu Hong	Huang Zongfu
Xiong Li		

CONTENTS

Learning About Chongqing 6~13

Geographical Location of Chongqing 8
The Four Seasons 8
Chongqing, an Ancient, Cultural City 9
Administrative Units 10
Millions on the Move 11
The Economic Center 11
Tourist and Cultural Resources 12

Tourist Attractions 16~91

A Visit in the City of Mountains 17~29

The New Three Gorges 31~43

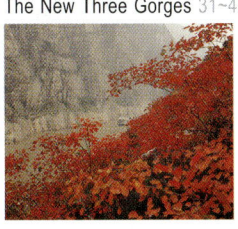

Lesser Three Gorges Tourist Area, Wushan 45~49

Three Gorges' Hinterland Scientific Exploration Tourist Area 51~55

Dazu Stone Carvings Tourist Area 57~63

Mt. Jinyun Tourist Area 65~69

Suburban Hot Spring and Lake Holiday Resort 71~75

Ecological Tourist Areas of Mt. Simian, Mt. Jinfo, and Wansheng Stone Forest 77~81

CONTENTS

Tourist Area of Mt. Fairy Maiden & Lotus Cave 83~84

Folklore Tourist Area of Qianjiang & Wujiang 85~91

VIP Former Residences, Memorial Halls 99~101

Cultural Groups, Recreational Places 102~107

Customs & Culture 93~107

The Arts 95~97
Sichuan Opera
Quyi
Xiushan Lantern Show
The Tu's Hand-Waving Dance

Folk Arts 97~98
Qijiang Farmer's Woodblocks
Tongliang Dragon Lantern
Rongchang Folding Fans

Tourism Information 108~152

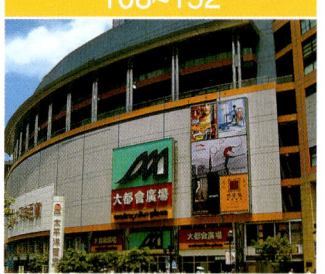

Transportation in the City of Mountains 111

Traffic in Downtown Chongqing 112

Transportation Along the Yangtze River 114

CONTENTS

Long-Distance Transportation 118

Rail Transport in Chongqing 118

Chongqing Airport 119

Shopping 121

Native Products, Medicinal Herbs 122

Native Products, Food 122

Native Products, Fruits 126

Native Products, Tea 127

Native Products, Liquor 128

Native Products, Wares 129

Sichuan Cuisine 132~139

Local Snacks 138

Tourist Accommodation 140

FAQ for Traveling in Chongqing 148~149

Travel Agencies 149~152

Learning About Chongqing

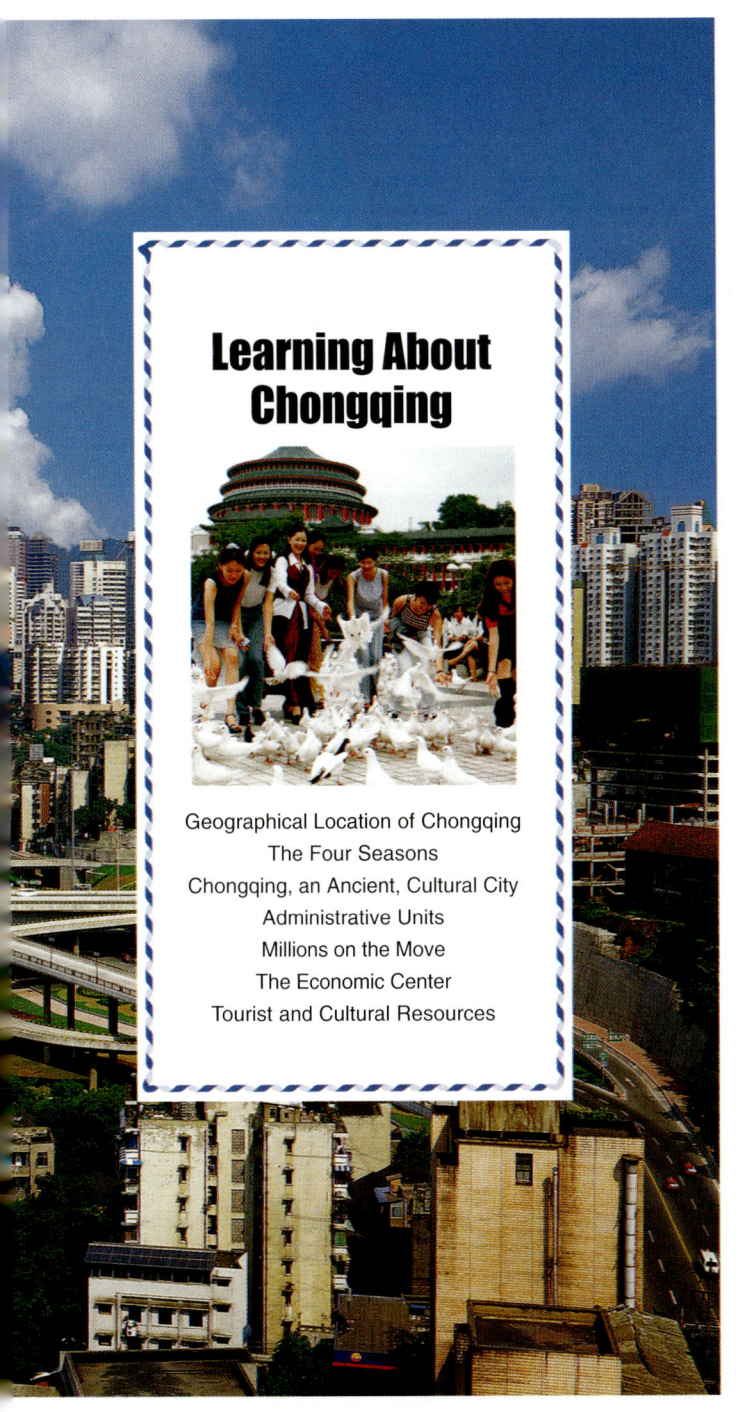

Geographical Location of Chongqing
The Four Seasons
Chongqing, an Ancient, Cultural City
Administrative Units
Millions on the Move
The Economic Center
Tourist and Cultural Resources

The City Flower

Camellia from the camellia family has a history of 2,000 years in Sichuan. Qixinhong, eight meters tall and 72 centimeters in diameter, is found by the Zhizi Bridge in Shigang, Banan District and believed to be 400 years old.

There are 73 species of camellia in Sichuan, 60 of which are found in Chongqing. The flower features long bloom, anti-pollution, and easy plantation, and can be found almost everywhere in the city: parks, scenic spots, courtyards, and buildings.

Learning About Chongqing

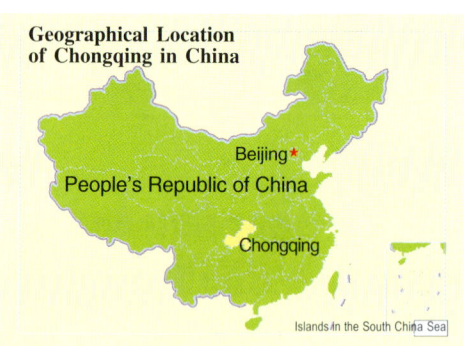

Geographical Location of Chongqing in China

Mean Temperature and Rainfall

Month	Temperature	Rainfall
Jan.	6 °C	19 mm
Feb.	9 °C	21 mm
Mar	14 °C	43 mm
Apr.	19 °C	72 mm
May	22 °C	155 mm
June	25 °C	165 mm
Juliy	29 °C	151 mm
Aug.	30 °C	141 mm
Sept.	26 °C	132 mm
Oct.	21 °C	99 mm
Nov.	15 °C	51 mm
Dec.	10 °C	25 mm

Geographical Location of Chongqing

Chongqing is located on the upper reaches of the Yangtze River in southwestern China. It covers 82,000 square kilometers in area, 470 kilometers from east to west and 450 kilometers from north to south, E105"11'~110"11', N28"10'~32"13', and touches the provinces of Hubei, Hunan, Guizhou, Sichuan, and Shaanxi.

The majority of Chongqing is along the banks of the Yangtze River, mainly hilly land at an average elevation of 400 meters. The north and south tilt to the Yangtze River valley. Featuring typical karst landformation, there are numerous limestone caves, hot springs, gorges, and ravines.

Chongqing has been known as the City of Mountains, and is located where the Jialing River empties into the Yangtze and hemmed in by mountains and rivers. It is especially enchanting when night falls.

The Four Seasons

Chongqing has a sub-tropical humid monsoon climate. The temperature in the early spring is unstable; the summer is long and hot; the autumn is cool and rainy; and the winter is mild, cloudy, and foggy.

The annual mean temperature is 18°C, and the record of the lowest temperature is 3.8°C on January 5, 1963. It is hot during July and August, 27 ~38°C, and the highest tempera-

Chongqing Harbor.

The People's Hall of Chongqing, imposing and grandeur, is a world-famous architecture and the pride of the city.

ture was 43.8°C on August 15, 1951. The temperature in the summer has been lowered down over the last few years thanks to the increase of vegetation and control of pollution.

Rain falls mostly at night in the summer and autumn, at an average of 1,000~1,100 millimeters a year.

Chongqing is known as the Capital of Fog. The unique topography and crisscrossing rivers produce huge fog in late autumn and early spring. The city is shredded by fog at an average of 68.3 days a year.

Sunlight is limited. The annual, average daily sunlight is only 1,259.5 hours. During July and August, Chongqing shares an average of 230 hours of sunlight a month, while the rest of the year 150 hours or so. Hemmed in by mountains on three sides with many gullies and ravines, the wind speed is relatively low. However, the wind is strong in thunderstorms in the summer, usually 10~27m /second.

Chongqing, an Ancient, Cultural City

Chongqing has a long history. Human activities were found as early as the Old Stone Age. Comparatively dense primitive villages were built during the New Stone Age. It was these residents that created the earliest civilization of Chongqing.

A powerful tribe known as Ba was established in Chongqing and its surrounding areas during the Xia, Shang, and Zhou (21th century~221 B.C.). Legend has it that Yu the Great divided China into nine states, and Ba belonged to the State of Liang. Historical records concerning Ba were found on the tortoise shell inscriptions.

The name of Chongqing has changed many times. In 316 B.C., the State of Qin conquered the State of Ba and made it a county. In 581 during the reign of Emperor Wendi

The City Tree

The Huangge Tree, or *Ficus virens var. sublancoolata*, from the banyan family, is the city tree of Chongqing.

The tree is vital with deep root, luxuriant foliage, and spreading branches. It grows fast, lives a long life, and is heat, humid, and pollution resistant. It grows healthily even on sheer cliffs.

A time-honored tree, Huangge can be found almost everywhere in Chongqing: streets, lanes, old walls, and mountain slopes.

A relief of the Han Dynasty (206 B.C.~A.D. 220).

An Ancient City

Chongqing has been reconstructed three times in history.

It was first established in 316, the 9th year during the reign of Emperor Huiwen of the Qin Dynasty, when the State of Ba was conquered.

During the Three Kingdoms Period (220~280), the city was enlarged in 226, known as Jiangzhou, whose boundary reached today's Tongyuan Gate.

Reconstruction was conducted during the early reign of Emperor Hongwu of the Ming Dynasty (1368~1644), when walls were built around the city, most of which were left behind.

of the Sui Dynasty (581~618), it was named Yuzhou. The name of Chongqing, meaning "double celebrations" in Chinese, was given in 1189, the 16th year of Emperor Chunxi's reign during the Jin Dynasty (1115~1234), which has remained unchanged.

Chongqing served as an important place for all dynasties beginning with the Qin Dynasty (221~207 B.C.). In 1921, it was made a commercial center; and in 1929, it became a city. May 5, 1935 saw the promotion of Chongqing as a municipality under the direct jurisdiction of the Kuomintang Government.

During the Anti-Japanese War (1935~45), the Kuomintang Government moved its capital to Chongqing in November 1937, and made it the "auxiliary capital" in 1940. So far, Chongqing had served as a capital three times.

Administrative Units

November 30, 1949 witnessed the liberation of Chongqing, which became the site of the Southwestern Military and Political Committee and a municipality under the direct jurisdiction of the CPC Central Committee. In July 1954, Chongqing was made a municipality under the jurisdiction of Sichuan Province. In 1983, it became China's first city specifically designated in the state plan. On March 14, 1997, the National People's Congress adopted the motion of making Chongqing a municipality under the direct jurisdiction of the Central Government, which was put into practice on June 18 the same year.

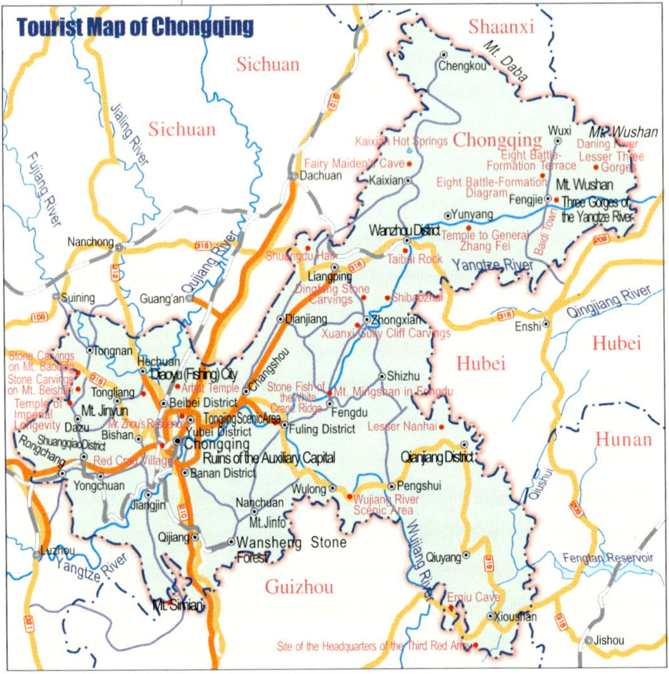

Learning About Chongqing

Chongqing covers an area of 82,400 square kilometers and has a population of 30.9045 million. It consists of 49 ethnic groups, the majority of which is the Tujia. By the end of 2001, it contained 15 districts, four county-level cities, and 21 counties, including minority autonomous counties.

Millions on the Move

The construction of the Three Gorges Water-Conservation Project has led to a large-scale resettlement of residents. According to the plan, 1.2 million residents from the Three Gorges area will resettle before 2009 when the project is completed. The three-stage resettlement project began in 1985, and 1.07 million Chongqing residents will find homes elsewhere.

The Economic Center

Chongqing is the largest city in West China. The Golden Watercourse of the Yangtze, the abundant natural resources, and the potential market have made Chongqing a center for

The Chang'an Suzuki production line.

industry and commerce as well as an economic center, a communication hub, and an inland port for the development of Southwest China and the upper reaches of the Yangtze River. Today, Chongqing is the country's important base for mechanical industry, chemical industry, pharmaceuticals, and instrument and meter making, and a production base for ordinary weapons. In recent years, the city has seen rapid development in hi-tech industry, food processing, and building materials.

The landforms and topographies and the pleasant climate offer favorable conditions for the development of agriculture and eco-agriculture, thus making Chongqing one of China's major production centers for commodity grain and porkers.

Chongqing has also seen a rapid development in the tertiary industry, including trade, tourism, finance, communication, IT, and real estate. The convenient transportation on land, water, and air has quickened up the pace of its economic development.

Taking a last look of his hometown.

A new village for resettlers.

Chongqing Tourist Guide

A terra-cotta story teller.

The Nickname of Ba

Traces of the Ba ancestors were found in the Dongting Lake area in northern Hunan Province, who later moved to the Hanjiang Plain, and then westward to Chongqing, Mt. Daba, and the Hanshui River region. Ancient Ba people took huge snakes and white tigers as their totems. Ba was the name of both the place and the tribe.

During their spare time.

Dr. Tea at Tongjufu.

Displaying his unique skill.

Tourist and Cultural Resources

The culture of Chongqing, better known as Ba and Yu, has been a component of the Chinese culture. According to many historical records, Yu the Great was born in Shiniu Village, Guangrou County, Wenshan County, Sichuan.

Chongqing's history of over 3,000 years has left behind countless cultural heritages, including the hometown of Qu Yuan and Wang Zhaojun, Zhouyiyuan in Fuling, the stone carvings of the Tang (617~907) and Song (960~1279) Dynasties in Dazu, and the Fishing City in Hechuan, where the battlefields of the Southern Song Dynasty (1127~1279) were preserved. Traces of past-dynasty men of letters, including Li Bai, Du Fu, Liu Yuxi, Su Shi, Lu You, and Guo Moruo, can also be found in Chongqing.

The people of Chongqing still remain the tradition that has

been carried out from generation to generation. There are greetings on Spring Festival, lantern shows on the 15th day of the first lunar month, sacrificial ceremonies to ancestors on the Pure Brightness Festival, temple fairs, and kite festivals, in addition to wedding ceremonies, funerals, cultural activities, and trade fairs.

The people of Chongqing do their own way in daily life due to the unique climate and geographical location, which is comparatively enclosed. They are frank yet somewhat rash, hospitable yet somewhat cunning, humorous yet somewhat uncouth, serious yet somewhat funny, casual yet somewhat irritable, and tolerant yet somewhat xenophobic.

The customs of Chongqing can be seen in its local operas, *quyi*, paintings, handicrafts, and cultural activities.

Chongqing takes pride in its rich tourism resources, which can be found in rolling mountains, crisscrossing rivers, long history, and brilliant culture, including the folklore of the ethnic groups, the culture of resettlement, the culture of the Three Gorges, the culture of the "auxiliary capital," and that of modern era.

The most well-known places of interest are the Three Gorges on the Yangtze River, the cliff carvings in Dazu, the landscape of the City of Mountains, Mt. Tushan, the sites of

Learning About Chongqing

The rainbow over the Three Gorges.

the famous personages of the Communist Party of China and Kuomintang, Mt. Jinfo, the natural pits and ground cracks, the lesser Three Gorges on the Daning River, and the ancient battlefields in the Fishing City in Hechuan. Among its hundreds of scenic spots, one was put on the list of the World Cultural Heritage, eight are state-level AAAA scenic spots, 12 are relics under state protection, six are national forest parks, two are state nature reserves, and four are national scenic spots; 24 provincial-level scenic spots, and five national centers for patriotic education; and 150 relics under municipal-level protection. The Chongqing Wild Animal Park, occupying 3.33 million square meters in area, leads China in species and number of wild an imals.

The simple, unique customs of Chongqing is another attraction, highlighted by Sichuan dishes. In 2000, Chongqing was cited as an Excellent Tourist City by the state.

Chongqing, ancient yet modern, is always ready to welcome friends from all parts of the world.

Residence

The city of Chongqing was built on the mountain slopes. Diaojiaolou, or houses made of timber or bamboo and suported by wooden stakes over ground, is a typical dwelling of old Chongqing.

In the past, most of the houses were built with timber or bamboo in hilly regions, while walls were built with wooden board or bamboowoven sheets reinforced with grass and mud. The space between the house and the ground can prevent the house from humidity caused by the weather, rainy and wet.

Today, modern high-rises have replaced Diaojiaolou, a rarity in downtown Chongqing. The best place to admire Diaojiaolou might be ancient towns.

Young ladies playing with doves.

The opening ceremony of the annual China Chongqing Three Gorges Tour.

Tanzhang Gorge at Wuqiao, Wanzhou District.

Tourist Attractions

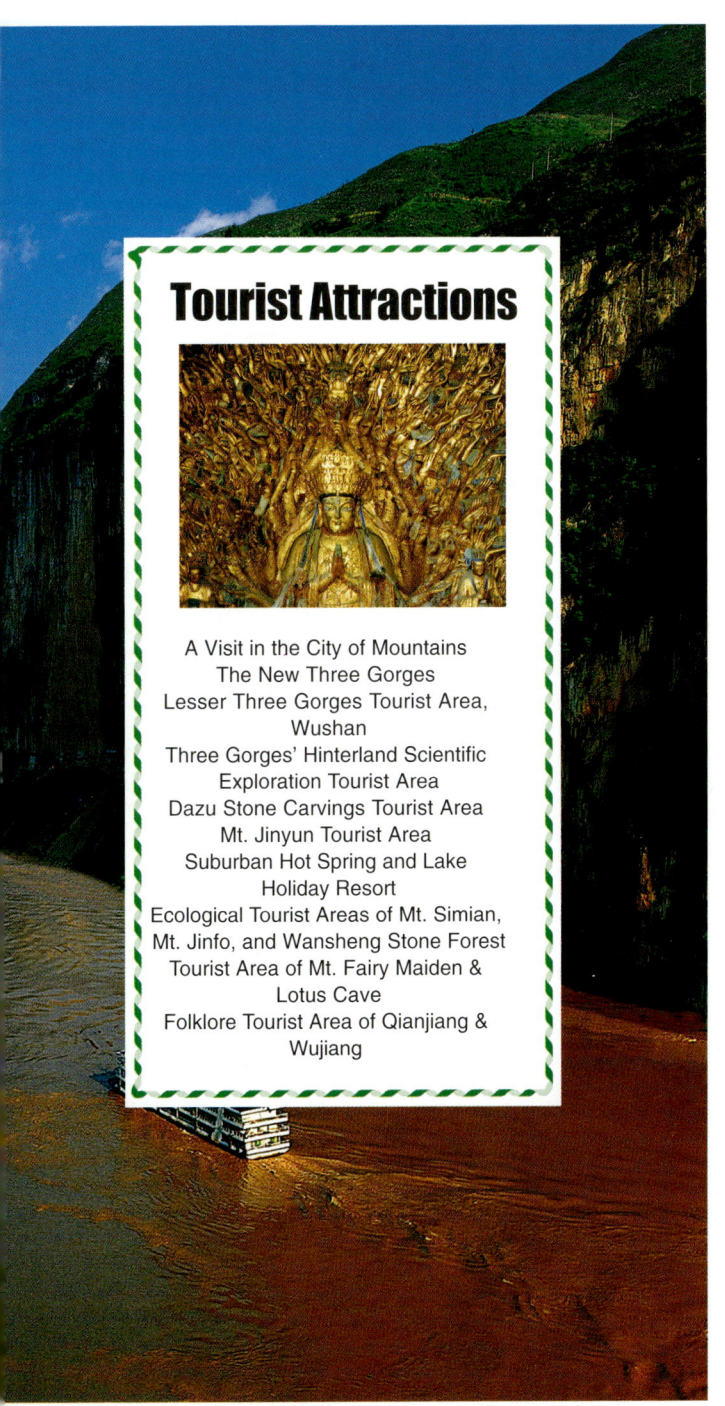

A Visit in the City of Mountains
The New Three Gorges
Lesser Three Gorges Tourist Area, Wushan
Three Gorges' Hinterland Scientific Exploration Tourist Area
Dazu Stone Carvings Tourist Area
Mt. Jinyun Tourist Area
Suburban Hot Spring and Lake Holiday Resort
Ecological Tourist Areas of Mt. Simian, Mt. Jinfo, and Wansheng Stone Forest
Tourist Area of Mt. Fairy Maiden & Lotus Cave
Folklore Tourist Area of Qianjiang & Wujiang

Tourist Attractions

A Visit in the City of Mountains

The tour includes the unique view of the City of Mountains, the night view of Chongqing, famous revolutionary sites, places of interest regarding to the Anti-Japanese War and the Auxiliary Capital, gardens, natural landscapes, and nature reserves.

The Night View of Chongqing

Yuzhong District, the major part of downtown Chongqing, features the natural landscapes of mountains and rivers. As night falls, Chongqing becomes a world of neon lights in the busy commercial center and street and bridge

Modern high-rises in Chongqing.

lamps, adding beauty to the myriad twinkling lights.

"You'll never experience real Chongqing if not admiring its night view," goes a local saying. Places worth visiting are the Red-Star Pavilion in Mt. Piba Park, the Grand-View Tower in Eling Park, Yikeshu, or the One Tree Only, on Mt. Nanshan, and Binjiang Road.

The Monument to Liberation

The Monument to Liberation stands at the crossroads of Minzu Road, Minquan Road, and Zourong Road in the Yuzhong District. It is one of the symbolic structures of the city. Erected on March 12, 1940, when Dr. Sun Yat-sen passed away, it was a wooden structure, nine meters tall, and was reinforced with concrete in August 1947. Its present name was inscribed by Liu Bocheng. The octagonal monument is now 35 meters in height and six meters in diameter. Winding stairs lead to the top.

The Central Shopping Square

The most bustling commercial center in Chongqing, the Central Shopping Square near the Monument to Liberation consists of the Pedestrian Mall and the Paradise for Shopping. The former covers 50,000 square meters in area, with high-rises, shops, movie theaters, recreational centers, grocery stores, bookstores, restaurants, and hotels. There are over 10 markets, each with an area of more than 1,000 square meters, such as the Chongqing Department Store, the New Century Department Store, and the Big Metropolis Plaza. The best place to enjoy local snacks is Bayi Road.

Water Character & the Lanterns Reflected in the Water

When the two rivers, Yangtze and Jialing, meet in Chongqing, they are in a shape of the Chinese character "巴". The night view was one of the 12 special scenes during Emperor Qianlong's reign of the Qing Dynasty. As night falls, the water character reflects the lanterns and lights along the banks, forming a fantastic world that can be hardly seen elsewhere.

Chongqing at night.

The Monument to Liberation.

Take Trolley Buses No. 401, 402, and 405 and Buses No. 103, 104, 105, 112, 215, 301, 304, 413, and 601.

The Big Metropolis Plaza at the Monument to Liberation square.

The People's Hall
Opening hours: 8:00~18:00. Ticket: 3 yuan. Tel: (0086-23) 6386 1137. Take Buses No. 103, 104, 105, 112, and 215.

Young painters.

Doing morning exercises.

Chongqing Harbor.

The People's Hall and the People's Square

Located at Xuetianwan, Renmin Rd., the People's Hall is an imposing, traditional Chinese building complex, one of the symbolic structures in Chongqing. In 1987, it ranked second among the 43 architectural projects of China on *The Comparative History of Architecture* in Britain.

Construction of the People's Hall began in 1951 and completed in 1954. It consists of four parts, the Hall, and buildings in the east, north, and south, with a total area of 66,000 square meters. The Hall has an area of 18,500 square meters, and is 65 meters tall. Its interior hall is 55 meters tall and 46.33 meters in diameter. The round hall is large enough to accommodate 5,000 people for various activities, such as important gatherings, ceremonies, and performances. The North and South Buildings are three-star hotels.

Resembling the outlook of the Temple of Heaven in Beijing, the Hall has a green, glaze-tiled roof, red pillars, white balustrades, and painted beams.

In front of the Hall is the People's Square built in June 1997, with an area of 40,000 square meters. The Square is laid with marble and has music fountains and evergreen lawns. Every day it attracts numerous visitors from home and abroad. As night falls, the local residents hold parties on the Square.

Both the People's Hall and People's Square are showcases for the image of Chongqing. To better display the city, the local government started the third phase of the construction of the Square, and the China Three Gorges Museum was built also on the Square, both in 2001.

The Golden Watercourse

After running 1,119 kilometers, the Jialing River on the left of Chaotianmen empties into the Yangtze River. The clear and green Jialing River water and the brown water of the Yangtze form a special view. The Yangtze becomes vast and mighty after accepting the Jialing, making it a golden watercourse of the river.

Chaotianmen & Chaotianmen Square

Chaotianmen, or South-Facing Gate, is located at the juncture of the Jialing and Yangtze Rivers in the Yuzhong District. It is the largest city gate among the 17 gated erected during the Ming Dynasty. In 1891, Chongqing was made a commercial center, and the Customs House was established at the Gate, which was pulled down in 1927 due to the construction of a ferry. A big fire in 1949 burnt the 2,000-kilometer region around the Gate to ruins, and the only thing left is the foundation.

The year 1998 saw the construction of the Square on the site of the Gate. Consisting of the Stair-Embankment, the View Square, and the Communication Square, Chaoyangmen Square occupies 50,000 square meters in area. It is where the largest harbor on the upper reaches of the Yangtze is

Tourist Attractions

located and the starting point of the trip to the Three Gorges. There are bus stations, hotels, restaurants, and a mall with a business area of nearly 400,000 square meters. The oceanliner-like Stair-Embankment is 48 meters wide and 320 meters long. The View Square covers an area of 15,000 square meters, and is the best place to admire the fantastic view along the Yangtze River. The title of the Square was inscribed by former president Jiang Zemin.

The imposing Chaotianmen Square.

The Three Gorges Square

Located in the central commercial area in Shapingba, the Three Gorges Square has an area of 21,600 square meters, and is a multi-functional square, where people can admire major miniature tourist attractions in the Three Gorges area, such as Chaotianmen, the White-Crane Ridge, the Ghost City, and the Water Conservation Project. A circulated water view, 1,600 cubic meters, displays the splendid scenery of the Three Gorges. There are also teahouses and an underground pedestrian mall, 25,000 square meters in area.

Chaotian Gate
Take Buses or Trolley Buses No. 401, 102, 103, 122, 114, and 215.

The Three Gorges Square
Take Buses or Trolley Buses No. 402, 404, 216, 217, and 218.

Manzi Tomb

Manzi was a general of the State of Ba during the Warring States Period some 2,000 years ago. His tomb was also known as the General's Tomb. It is located by the Lotus Pond in Qixingyan, Yuzhong District. The gravestone was inscribed by Dan Maoxin in the early years of the Republic of China.

The Tomb of Manzi

According to a local, historical record, in the late Eastern Zhou Dynasty (770 ~ 256 B.C.), General Manzi asked the State of Chu for military support to put down a civil strife with an offer of three cities. The revolt was suppressed, but the General could hardly bear to cede his cities, and cut his throat to show his apologies. The king was moved and held a grand funeral for the General.

Nobody knows the exact time the tomb was built, but it was rebuilt in 1922.

The Tomb of Manzi
Take Buses No. 413, 601, and 109, or Trolley Buses No. 401, 402, and 405, and get off at Qixingyan.

Hongyan Revolutionary Memorial Hall

The Red-Crag, or Hongyan, Village in the Pingba District has made great contributions to the founding of the New China. In the 1930s, it was a private garden of Madam Rao Guomo. In 1939, it served as the office of the South Bureau of the Central Committee of the Chinese Communist Party as well as the headquarters of the Eighth Route Army. During the eight-year Anti-Japanese War, many famous Chinese Communist Party leaders, such as Zhou Enlai, Dong Biwu, and Ye Jianying, worked and lived here. During the Chongqing Negotiation, Comrade Mao Zedong spent 41 days and nights in the village, which has become world famous for its remarkable contribution to

The former office of Mao Zedong in the Red-Crag Village.

Hongyan Revolutionary Memorial Hall

Opening hours: 8:30~17:00. Through ticket: 15 yuan. Take Buses No. 104, 215, 216, 217, and 219.

The CPC South Bureau & No. 50 Zengjiayan

Opening hours: 8:30~21:00. Ticket: 2 yuan. Take Buses or Trolley Buses No. 103, 104, 105, 108, 112, 401, 405, and 601, and get off at Shangqingsi.

A bronze statue of Zhou Enlai

President's Residence

During the Anti-Japanese War, the KMT established its Central Political College in today's Xiaoquan Hotel in the Jiulongpo District. The room No. 1 is the former residence of then President Chiang Kai-shek of the college. The one-story, Western-style building was built by Chen Guofu, director of the Education Department of the college.

Guiyuan

Opening hours: 8:30~17:00. Take Buses or Trolley Buses No. 103, 104, 105, 108, 112, 401, 405, and 601, and get off at Shangqingsi.

the Chinese revolution. Today, it is a center for patriotic education and a relic under state protection.

The office building of the Eighth Route Army, No. 13 in the Village, is a three-story wooden structure, 800 square meters in area. The first floor is the office; the second floor are the offices and bedrooms of Mao Zedong and Zhou Enlai, where the manuscript of *Snow*, a famous poem of Mao Zedong, is still on display; the third floor are also offices, where top secrets were sent to the central government in Yan'an. Viewers can learn about the life and work at that time through the photos and articles in the building.

In June 2001, the Hongyan Revolutionary Memorial Hall at 52 Red-Crag Village was opened. There are exhibition halls, the Wax Hall of the Chongqing Negotiation, and a multifunction hall.

No. 50 Zengjiayan

Also known as Zhou's Mansion, Zenjiayan is located in the Yuzhong District. In the winter of 1938, the delegation of the Communist Party of China (CPC) moved from Wuhan to Chongqing. To make work convenient, Comrade Zhou Enlai rented this house in his own name. It served as the major office of the South Bureau of the CPC.

The house is located at the end of a small lane. On the right side is the residence of Dai Li, director of the Kuomintang (KMT) Bureau of Military Investigation and Statistics, while on the left side a KMT police station.

The CPC delegation rented the first and third floors, and the rest were inhabited by the KMTs.

The offices of Dong Biwu and Ye Jianying are on the second and third floors. In August 1945, Comrade Mao Zedong came to negotiate with Chiang Kai-shek, during which time he interviewed personages at home and abroad in the meeting room on the basement. Zhou Enlai often met personages from all walks of life as well as Chinese and foreign reporters. In March 1947, the KMT special agents sealed the place, and the CPC staff withdrew.

In June 2001, the local government decided to build a 1,400-square-meter square in front of the building. A bronze statue of Zhou Enlai was erected in the middle of the square in 1988.

Guiyuan

Located at 65 Zhongshan Road Fourth, Yuzhong District, Guiyuan is the former residence of the KMT General Zhang Zhizhong. In August 1945, during the Chongqing Negotiation,

Tourist Attractions

Mr. Zhang offered his place as both an office and a meeting place for Mao Zedong.

Guiyuan is a small, independent courtyard with the gate facing the street. There are two sweet-scented osmanthus in the courtyard, hence its name. The main building is where Mao Zedong and Zhou Enlai negotiated with the KMTs and signed the *October 10 Agreement*. The second floor are the offices and sitting rooms of Mao Zedong and Zhou Enlai, where photos and reports on the negotiation are still displayed.

In 1977, Guiyuan was opened to public. Three years later, it was designated as a relic under provincial protection, and today, it is a relic under state protection.

Ruins of the Auxiliary Capital

Mt. Huangshan in the Nan'an District is famous for its beautiful, natural landscapes. In 1938, Japan bombed Chongqing. To get rid of the bomb as well as the heat in summer, Chiang Kai-shek built an official residence on Mt. Huangshan, and lived in the building named Yunxiu, while Soong Mei-ling, his wife, lived in Songting, or Pine Hall.

Between the two buildings there is an air-raid shelter especially built for Chiang Kai-shek and his wife. Not far from Yunxiu is a one-story building in traditional Chinese style, known as Straw Pavilion. In 1945, General George Catlett Marshall, special envoy of then American president Harry S. Truman, came to "mediate the dispute between the CPC and KMT," and lived in the pavilion.

Also on Mt. Huangshan are Kung's Mansion, Lianqing Building of the American Military Consulting Delegation, and a primary school for the children of the Anti-Japanese War martyrs, as well as former foreign embassies and villa blocks.

Linyuan

Linyuan was the official residence of Lin Sen, president of the KMT government during the Anti-Japanese War. It is located on Shuanghe Street at the foot of Mt. Gele and was built in 1939. Linyuan was originally built for Chiang Kai-shek. When he came to congratulate the completion of the building, Lin Sen rained praises on the building, and Chiang gave his adhesion right away to Lin as a gift. Hence the name.

In 1943, Lin died in a traffic accident, and Chiang moved to Linyuan. Building No. 1 was for Chiang, Building No. 2 for Chiang's wife, and Building No. 3 was Chiang's office building. The former residence of Lin Sen was Building No. 4.

At 3:00 a.m. on November 30, 1949, Chiang left Linyuan for Chengdu. Today, Linyuan is a relic under municipal protection, with scenic spots, such as the Kai-Shek and Mei-

The Site of Xinhua Daily

Located at 204 Minsheng Road, Yuzhong District, it is a black, three-story building where *Xinhua Daily* was run in August 1940. The title was inscribed by Mao Zedong. It was a distribution center for CPC's newspaper and progressive publications and a liaison office for revolutionary personages.

Xinhua Daily was established in October 1937 in Nanjing, and was published on January 11, 1938 in Wuhan. It was the only CPC newspaper published in the districts under KMT's power. In February 1947, it was forced to close by the KMT.

The well-preserved site of the Auxiliary Capital.

Site of the Auxiliary Capital

Opening hours: 8:30~17:00. Take Bus No. 384, the cable car, or a minibus at Shangxin St.

Linyuan

Take Bus No. 212.

Mao Zedong and Chiang Kai-shek during the Chongqing Negotiation.

Mao Zedong in Chongqing

On August 28, 1945, Mao Zedong flied from Yan'an to Chongqing to participate in the KMT-CPC Negotiation. At the night he arrived, Chiang Kai-shek invited Mao, Zhou Enlai, and Wang Ruofei to dinner at Linyuan. Mao stayed overnight in Building No. 2. Early next morning, Mao took a stroll in the garden and came across Chiang. Mao and Chiang then sat by a stone table and talked. Mao left Linyuan the next day.

The Soul of the Red Crag, a fragment of the large sculptures in Mt. Gele Martyr's Cemetery

Bai's Mansion.

The Zhazidong Dregs Cave Concentration Camp.

ling's Buildings, Marshall's Mansion, the Tomb of Lin Sen, and the Negotiation Table.

Kung's Mansion

Located by the Huxiao Spring in the Southern Spring Park and built in 1939, the Kung's Mansion was the former residence of H. H. Kung, financial minister of the KMT. It was built in Chinese and Western styles. On the left is the former ballroom of the Kung's; and articles used by Kung's and photos of the three sisters of the Soong's are displayed in the room on the right. At the back of the main building is an air-raid shelter against Japanese bomb.

On the hillside left of the main building is the former residence of Kung Lingyi, the second daughter of H. H. Kung, and on the right side is a drill ground. One kilometer up along the mountain path is Jianwen Peak.

Mt. Gele Martyr's Cemetery

The foot of Mt. Gele, Shapingba District, used to be the headquarters, the radio station, and the prisons of the KMT Bureau of Military Investigation and Statistics. The Sino-American Cooperation Organization (SACO) was also founded here in the late World War II. The year 1954 saw the establishment of the Martyr's Cemetery and the monument, which were renamed in 1984, and are now relics under state protection and a center for patriotic education.

The SACO, an intelligence organization between the KMT government and the US, covers an area of 10 square kilometers in the covered mountain valley. There were offices, dorms, restaurants, ballroom, halls, the arsenal, the Zhazidong Dregs Cave Concentration Camp, and 20 prisons, big and small. After the South Anhui Incident in 1941, General Ye Ting, commander of the New Fourth Army, was imprisoned here, and some famous CPC members, including Luo Shiwen, Che Yaoxian, and Jiang Zhujun, as well as patriotic high-ranking military officials, such as Yang Hucheng and Huang Xiansheng, were killed here. Prior to its withdrawal from China's mainland on November 27, 1949, the KMT massacred more than 300 revolutionary personages, known as the November 27 Massacre.

There are over 30 relic sites in the Cemetery, including the Red Crag Square of the Soul, the Bai's Mansion, the Execution Ground at Songlipo, the Zhazidong Dregs Cave Concentration Camp, the Stone Tablets to praise the Martyrs, the Martyr's Sculpture District, the Former Residence of Dai Li at Yangjiashan, the Secret Prison of Hongluchang, where Generel Ye Ting was imprisoned, and the Meiyuan, the former office of the deputy director of the SACO. The Red Crag Square of the

Soul, 3,000 square meters in area, is now a place for important gatherings and activities. In front of the Square are sculptured martyrs and tombs. On the right is an exhibition hall.

Arhats Temple

Situated on Minzu Road, Yuzhong District, the Arhats Temple is one of the major Buddhist temples in the regions mainly inhabited by the Han people in China, and is the site of the Chongqing Buddhist Association.

Also known as Zhiping Temple, it was first built in the Tang Dynasty and enlarged during Emperor Zhiping's reign of the Northern Song Dynasty. In 1752, the 17th year of Emperor Qianlong's reign during the Qing Dynasty, it was rebuilt into a temple to worship the Dragon God. In 1885, the 11th year during Emperor Guangxu's reign of the Qing Dynasty, it was reconstructed and renamed Arhats Temple, where the Hall of Arhats was built with 500 clay figurines of arhats. Unfortunately, the Temple was destroyed by the Japanese bomb in 1942 but later rebuilt.

On the 20-meter-long cliff in the temple there are more than 400 Buddhist statues carved during the Song Dynasty, among which the Sleeping Nirvana and the Goddess of Mercy are pretty much the same as the style of the stone carvings on Mt. Baoding in Dazu.

Among the artistic treasures of Buddhism in the Mahavira Hall, the most valuable are the three bronze statues of the Western Saints made in the Ming Dynasty and the mural of Sakyamuni's trip to a monastery from Myanmar. Moreover, the temple also collects a great number of Buddhist scriptures in Sanskrit and Tibetan languages, ancient books, and calligraphy and paintings, most of which are of the Tang and Ming Dynasties.

There are 524 clay figurines of arhats in the Hall of Arhats, vivid, and meticulously made, and worshipped by Buddhists.

There is a restaurant in the Temple, which is famous for vegetable dishes.

Temple of Benevolent Clouds

Lying at the foot of Mt. Shizi (Lion) in Xuantan Temple, Nan'an District, the Temple was first built in the Tang Dynasty and rebuilt during the reign of Emperor Qianlong of the Qing Dynasty. In 1927, *Dharmacarya* Yun Yan raised funds for the expansion of the temple, which was renamed Benevolent Clouds, the only Buddhist temple for both monks and nuns in China.

Benevolent Clouds is unique in style, both Chinese and Western, among Buddhist temples in China. Its main buildings include the Mahavira Hall, the Samantabhadra Hall, the Three-Sage Hall, the Tripitaka Pavilion, and the Drum-Bell Tower.

Among its rich collections, the most famous are the Jade Buddha, the Vajrasana stone pillar, the Thousand-Buddha robe, the Buddhist scriptures, and *bodhi* tree, which was transplanted from India 60 years ago. The Buddhist scriptures, a copy of the Song Dynasty, contain 6,362 volumes. There

Mt. Gele Martyr's Cemetery
Opening hours: 8:30~17:00. Take Buses No. 215, 217, 221.

Arhats Temple

The main hall of the Arhats Temple

Arhats Temple
Opening hours: 8:00~18:00. Take Trolley Bus No. 401 and Buses No. 103, 104, 105, 111, 112, and 122, and get off at Xiaoshizi.

Temple of Benevolent Clouds
Opening hours: 8:00~18:00. It is an easy access to walk along the southern bank of Binjiang Road.

The Jade Buddha
The Mahavira Hall in the Temple of Benevolent Clouds enshrines a jade statue of Sakyamuni, 1.87m in height and 1,500kg in weight. The jade Buddha, moved from Myanmar in 1931, is one of the four largest jade Buddhas in China. In front of the jade Buddha there are four flags hung down, with the full text of the Cajracchedika-sutra.

Cave of Immortality
Opening hours: 8:00~18:00.
Take Buses No. 347 and 384.

Cave of Immortality, the most famous sacred place for Taoism in eastern Sichuan.

The gate of Huayan Temple.

Huayan Temple
Opening hours: 8:00~18:00.
Take Bus No. 222.

1,000-year-old Huayan Cave.

are also other collections, such as classics of the Buddhist sutra, golden embroidery of the images of the Buddha, ancient finger paintings and calligraphy, and the original copies of images and photos of the Buddha published in Japan.

Cave of Immortality

Located on Mt. Laojun, two kilometers south of the Nan'an District, the Cave was built in the Tang Dynasty, known as the Guanghua Temple. It was changed into a Taoist temple and renamed Taiji Palace, or Cave of Immortality, in 1581, the ninth year of Emperor Wanli's reign during the Ming Dynasty. Reconstructions and expansions were undergone during the reigns of Emperors Daoguang, Tongzhi, and Guangxu of the Qing Dynasty. It consists of nine halls, each of which was meticulously structured on the mountain slope.

On the first day, the 15th day of the first lunar month, or on the Festival of Pure Brightness, numerous people come to worship.

Huayan Temple

Located on Mt. Dalao in Huayan Town, Jiulongpo District, the Temple was named after a cave in the south of the temple. Nobody knows the exact time of its establishment, but records were found concerning its reconstructions during the reigns of Emperors Kangxi, Daoguang, and Tongzhi of the Qing Dynasty. The Temple covers 160,000 square meters in area, with a floor space of 16,000 square meters. The cliff behind the Temple measures more than 330 meters high, and the Temple is secluded in the shade of lush pines and bamboo.

The titles of the Temple and the cave were inscribed in 1988 by Zhao Puchu, former president of the China Buddhist Association. In 1937, a Buddhist institute was established in the temple, attracting Buddhists and scholars from 20 countries in Europe and Asia.

Huayan Temple consists of two parts, the Greater and the Lesser. The main halls, including the Mahavira, the Founder of Buddhism, and the Goddess of Mercy, are wooden-and-brick structures. The Mahavira Hall enshrines 16 wooden figurines of ancestral Buddhas. The Temple has a rich collection of jade Buddhist statues from India, bronze, jade, stone, wood, and clay figurines of Buddhas, and a model of the Giant Golden Pagoda.

The Lesser is the Huayan Cave, facing the Temple on the other side of the lake.

Tourist Attractions

Tushan Temple

Standing on top of Mt. Tushan, the Temple was first built in the Tang Dynasty and was changed into a Genuine Prowess Palace during the reign of Emperor Jiajing of the Ming Dynasty. It was made a Buddhist temple in the ninth year of Emperor Wanli's reign during the Ming Dynasty, and was rebuilt and enlarged several times during the Ming Dynasty and the early period of the Republic of China. Today, the Temple has eight halls.

Tushan Temple.

The Mosque

The mosque, 4,500 square meters in area, is located on Zhongxing Road, Yuzhong District. Built during the reign of Emperor Wanli of the Ming Dynasty, it consisted of three parts, West, North, and South. In 1940, the South was destroyed by the Japanese bombs, and was rebuilt two years later. Then, the North and South joined the West.

In 1982, the Mosque was completely reconstructed, with green, Arabian-style top symbolized by the moon and stars. The hall, supported by four pillars, looks grandeur and solemn with harmoniously painted walls. The mosque enshrines the Islamic scriptures; and *ahung* hosts religious activities here. On each Islamic festive occasion, devotees gather here, praying and citing scriptures. Friday is a regular time for the meeting.

The Mosque has a guesthouse and a restaurant, and it is the site of the Chongqing Islamic Association.

The Mosque
Take Buses No. 109, 301, 303, and 306.

St. Joseph's Church

Catholicism was introduced to Chongqing in 1858, the eighth year during Emperor Xianfeng's reign of the Qing Dynasty. St. Joseph's Church on Minsheng Road, Yuzhong District, covers 1,700 square meters in area, 500 square meters of which is the main hall, large enough to hold 1,000 people. The statues of Jesus, the Blessed Virgin Mary, and Joseph are enshrined right in the middle, and 14 oil paintings of Jesus' cultivation are found on the walls. Three Masses are held on Sunday. More than 1,000 Catholics gather in the church during major Catholic activities.

St. Joseph's Church
Take Buses No. 413 and 601 or Trolley Bus No. 401.

St. Joseph's Church, a major Catholic church in Chongqing, was built during Emperor Guangxu's reign, Qing Dynasty.

The Bell Tower

The year 1917 witnessed the erection of the Cross Bell Tower under the supervision of a French priest. The Tower stands 36 meters in height, and has three pendent bells and a clock. The Hall was destroyed during the Anti-Japanese Wall but the Tower was fortunately undamaged.

Chongqing Christian Church

The Christian Church at 96 Ciqi Street, where the Monument to Liberation stands, is where major religious activities are held to celebrate festivals, such as Christmas and Easter. The Christian Church was established in 1925, large enough to accommodate 1,000 people, and was destroyed during the Anti-Japanese War. It was rebuilt with donations in 1943 and removed in May 1998.

The Grand-View Tower in Eling Park.

Eling Park

Eling Park is situated on the mountain ridge of the peninsula, Yuzhong District. It was so named because of the

Eling Park.

Eling, Fotu Pass Parks
Opening hours: 8:00~22:00.
Take Buses or Trolley Buses No. 109, 412, 413, 418, 412, 421, 402, and 403.

The Red-Star Pavilion in Mt. Pipa Park.

Mt. Pipa Park
Opening hours: 8:00~22:00.
Take Buses or Trolley Buses No. 105, 413, 418, 601, 401, and 405, get off at Wenhuagong, and walk for five minutes.

shape of the mountain ridge, where the Yangtze and Jialing Rivers run through.

Also known as Liyuan, the Park was first built during the reign of Emperor Xuantong of the late Qing Dynasty. In 1958, the municipal government reconstructed the Park, building towers and pavilions and planting trees, plants, and flowers, and named it as Eling.

The layout of the Park features that of the gardens in Suzhou. Major scenic spots include the Potted-Landscape Garden, the Flying Pavilion, the Rope Bridge, the Grand-View Tower, the Long Corridor, and the Terrace to Admire the Landscapes of Mountains and Rivers. There are also places of historic interest, such as the former residence of the Chiang's during the Anti-Japanese War and the former embassies of Australia and Turkey.

The best place to get a panoramic view of the whole city, especially the night view of Chongqing, and the splendor of the two rivers, is the Grand-View Tower, the very top of the peninsula.

Fotu Pass Park

Fotu Pass Park, a neighbor of Eling Park, was so named because of the Buddhist carvings on cliffs.

Fotu Pass is the narrowest point, less than 1,000 meters from north to south, between the Yangtze and Jialing Rivers. It was built by Prefect Li Yan 1,700 years ago. It used to be a thoroughfare between Chongqing and Chengdu and a place of military, transportation importance.

Covering an area of 320,000 square meters, the Pass rises among the rolling hills, dangerous, imposing, and precipitous. The many places of historic interest and scenic spots in the Park make it an ideal place for the local residents to enjoy their spare time. Standing on the summit, one can see the rivers and the sheer cliffs along the banks. It is also known as Futu because the scenery resembles the fabled fairyland of immortals in Penglai, Shandong Province.

Mt. Pipa Park

Located on Mt. Pipa (Loquat), Zhongshan Road in the Yuzhong District, the Park is 345 meters above sea level, the highest place in the old district of Chongqing. It used to be a private garden, known as Wang's Garden, of Wang Lingji, former governor of Sichuan of the National Government. In 1955, it was renamed Mt. Pipa Park and opened to public.

The mountain paths of Pipa zigzag among the luxuriant bamboo grooves, flowers, and plants; and the air is fresh. There are scenic spots, such as the Red-Star Pavilion, Crape Myrtle Park, and Yingcui Park.

The Red-Star Pavilion faces Eling Park on the other side of the city. It is another place to enjoy the panoramic view and the night view of Chongqing.

Shanhu (Coral) Park

Located at Caiyuanba, Yuzhong District along the banks of the Yangtze, Shanhu was established in December 1997, and has an area of 100,000 square meters, of which 58,000 square meters are greened up with peaches, willows, cotton roses,

Tourist Attractions

camellias, wintersweets, and magnolias. The Park is also a showcase of the cultures, ancient and modern, of Chongqing, which can be seen in tourist attractions, such as the Light Pillar of the Century, the Culture Square, and the Giant Galloping Dragon. Strolling in the Park, one can see high-rises on the peninsula in the City of Mountains, listen to the waves of the Yangtze, and admire the imposing Yangtze Bridge.

The Coral Park.

South Korean Provisional Government

The provisional government of South Korea is a government-in-exile for the long-term anti-Japanese independent movement in China. It was established in April 1919 in Shanghai, and moved to Chongqing in March 1939. The members of the organization returned to their motherlands after August 1945 when Tokyo proclaimed unconditional surrender. In August 1995, both governments of China and South Korea agreed to resume and open to public the site of the provisional government, which displays 468 articles and 150 relics and materials.

The site of the South Korean Provisional Government.

Mt. Nanshan Scenic Area

Located along the southern banks of the Yangtze River, the tourist area ranges from the Tongluo Gorge in the north to the Jinzhu Gully in the south, with a total area of 2,500 hectares. The average elevation is 400 meters, and the highest peak, the Chuntian Spring Range, stands 681.5 meters above sea level. These mountains and peaks form a natural green barrier to safeguard Chongqing.

The Tourist Area has rich tourism resources with mountains, rivers, forests, springs, waterfalls, gorges, and flowers, in addition to religious structures of Buddhism, Taoism,

Mt. Nanshan Scenic Area

Take Buses No. 347 and 384 or the cable car to Mt. Nanshan.

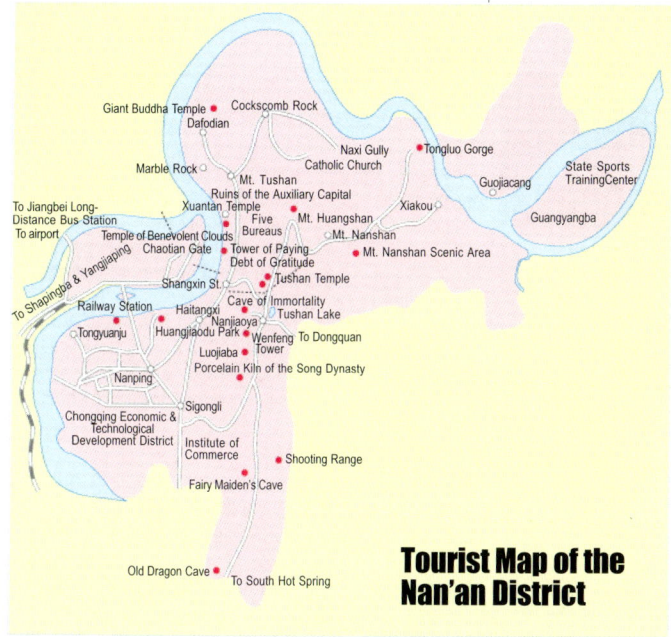

Tourist Map of the Nan'an District

The Rose Garden in Mt. Nanshan.

Mt. Nanshan Park.

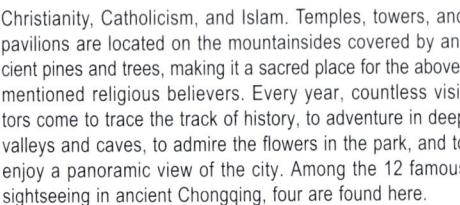
The giant pandas in the zoo.

Chongqing Zoo
Opening hours: 8:00~18:00. Take Buses or Trolley Buses No. 412, 413, 416, 419, 223, 403, and 404.

Mt. Gele Forest Park
Take Buses No. 215, 217, 221, and 227, get off at Lieshimu, and shift a minibus or cable car to the Park.

The Giant Golden Eagle.

Christianity, Catholicism, and Islam. Temples, towers, and pavilions are located on the mountainsides covered by ancient pines and trees, making it a sacred place for the above-mentioned religious believers. Every year, countless visitors come to trace the track of history, to adventure in deep valleys and caves, to admire the flowers in the park, and to enjoy a panoramic view of the city. Among the 12 famous sightseeing in ancient Chongqing, four are found here.

Mt. Nanshan Park
Mt. Nanshan Park is located in the Mt. Nanshan Scenic Area. It has an area of 170,000 square meters, and consists of three parts, the Rose Garden, the Wintersweet and Osmanthus Garden, and the Orchid Garden. It is a gathering place for over 100 species of azaleas, 50 species of camellias, Japanese flowering cherries, British osmanthus, and Mexican chrysanthemums. In addition, it is the largest plantation for 10 famous flowers of Chongqing, including Chinese flowering crab-apple, cherry, osmanthus, wintersweet, azalea, gardenia, magnolia, crape myrtle, and orchid.

Chongqing Zoo
Located at Yangjiaping, Jiulongpo District, the Zoo covers an area of 410,000 square meters, and was first established in 1953, known as the Western District Park. It was renamed Chongqing Zoo in 1958.

Embraced by mountains and hills with luxuriant bamboo grooves, the Zoo is home to more than 2,000 animals in 120 species, including the wild carnivorous, the herbivorous, primates, birds, the amphibious, and reptiles. The rare species include giant panda, lesser panda, golden monkey, South China tiger, elephant, hippopotamus, and takins.

Mt. Gele Forest Park
Located on Mt. Gele in the Shapingba District, the Forest Park served as a barrier in ancient, western Chongqing. Its main peak towers 693 meters above sea level.

With rolling hills, magnificent mountains, and beautiful landscape, Mt. Gele is enchanting with such scenic spots as the Horse's-Hoof Well, the Dragon Spring Well, the Smart Spring, and the Long Corridor of Sculptures of the Ba Culture, which consists of thousands of stone carvings representing the history and culture of the Bas. There are facilities for sports, such as rock climbing and skating in the Forest Park.

Also found here is the Exhibition Hall of the Auxiliary Capital Culture, with an area of 200 square meters, where people can learn about major events and famous personages through 370 photos and written materials about the Auxiliary Capital.

Giant Golden Eagle Park
The Park, next to the Wintersweet and Osmanthus Garden, is located at the foot of Yaoying Peak, 669 meters above sea level, the second highest peak in Mt. Nanshan.

The Giant Golden Eagle, 22 meters tall, faces east and stands on a 10-meter-high red conch. Coated with gold, it

Tourist Attractions

glimmers in the brilliant sunlight during the daytime and presents a special charm in lights at night. Within the sculpture there are spiral stairs leading to the top. There are also terraces on the spots of the wings, where visitors can have a bird's-eye view of the city and the night view of the City of Mountains.

Ancient Town of Ciqikou

Located along the banks of the Jialing River, Shapingba District, the town has been famous for porcelain products since the Ming and Qing Dynasties. Over 20 kilns of 2,000 years old have been discovered in the town. Baolun Temple, well preserved, was built during 1064 and 1067, the reign of Emperor Zhiping of the Northern Song Dynasty.

The ancient town of Ciqikou.

A temple fair at Ciqikou.

Ciqikou is a miniature of old Chongqing. It has drawn numerous visitors with its unadored, ancient streets laid with stone slabs, traditional houses of the Ming and Qing styles, old-fashioned teahouses, and authentic local snacks.

Sanduoqiao Village Egret Nature Reserve

Located in Baishiyi Town, Jiulongpo District, the Sanduoqiao Village Egret Nature Reserve is the first of its kind in China. The natural environment, tranquil and rich in bamboo, offers favorable conditions for more than 20,000 egrets, depicting a unique scroll of natural beauty.

February and March are the best season to admire the picturesque scenery when the mountain slopes are covered by peach flowers in full blossom and egrets fly over the green sea of bamboo. There are also other scenic spots, such as the Fish and Crane Garden, the Lidi Garden, and the Garden of Lotus Ponds. Despite admiring egrets and the natural splendor, visitors can also participate in various activities, such as fishing, chess, photography, and farm work, and enjoy lotus delicacies.

Tieshanping Forest Park

Located on the Tongluo Mountain Range 20 kilometers east of Guanyin Bridge, Jiangbei District, the Park is 500 meters above sea level and covers 10 square kilometers in area. The mountain has a flat, vast top, with fresh air and pleasant climate. Standing here, one can see the Yangtze River running through the precipitous Tongluo Gorge, a vital passage in eastern Chongqing and a place of military importance in ancient times.

In the Forest Park there are an education center for the dissemination of national defense, the Ostrich Garden, the Grass Garden, and the Hot Spring Pools. The hot spring, 38°C, produces 1,000 tons of water a day and contains high hydrogen sulphide and elements, such as fluorine, strontium, and boron, which can cure skin diseases.

Egrets

Measuring 50cm in length, egrets have long, snow-white feathers. In the spring and summer, they play by lake sides and rice fields. They live in group, and eat small fish. The mating season is from the spring to August. The southern part of the Yangtze River and the Hainan Islands offer ideal conditions for these birds.

The Tomb of Ming Yuzhen

The Tomb of Ming Yuzhen at Shangheng Street, Jiangbei District, is a relic under municipal protection. An exhibition hall was established by the Tomb.

Ming Yuzhen is a famous leader of the peasant's uprising in the late Yuan Dynasty as well as the founder of the State of Xia, one of the capitals as which Chongqing served in history. Unearthered from the Tomb are a gold cup, two silver ingots, and a large number of silk products. On the gravestone are 1,000 Chinese characters recording the life of Ming Yuzhen, which are of high value for the study of history.

Tourist Attractions

The New Three Gorges

The travel route from Chongqing to Yichang has been attractive for the brilliant culture and numerous places of interest, especially magnificent view of the Three Gorges along the Yangtze River. The most famous tourist attractions include Zhouyi Garden in Fuling, the inscriptions on the White-Crane Ridge, Mt. Mingshan in Fengdu, Shibaozhai, Temple to General Zhang Fei, Baidi Town, the ruins of the Three Kingdoms, the Eight Battle-Formation Diagram, the Three Gorges, the Memorial Hall to Qu Yuan, the Three Gorges Water Conservation Project, and the tomb and temple to the Yellow Emperor. This scenic area is a national park for sightseeing, scientific and cultural research, and architectural investigation.

The 6,380-kilometers-long Yangtze River is the longest river in China and the third longest river in the world. Descending from Mt. Tanggula in Qinghai Province, the river sweeps from west to east through Qinghai, Tibet, Yunnan, Sichuan, Chongqing, Hubei, Hunan, Jiangxi, Anhui, Jiangsu, and Shanghai, and empties itself into the East China Sea. It has many tributaries, free from frozen, making it a golden waterway in the country.

The Yangtze River from Yibin, Sichuan, to Yichang, Hubei, is known as Chuanjiang. The lower reaches suddenly narrow down and are sandwiched by sheer cliffs along the banks, creating one of nature's most fantastic sights, the Three Gorges. Chongqing is the best starting point to enjoy the beauty of the Three Gorges.

The 193-kilometer-long Three Gorges consist of the Qutang, eight kilometers long, the Wuxia, 44 kilometers long, and the Xiling, 76 kilometers long. It starts from Baidi, Fengjie County of Chongqing, in the west, and ends at Nanjin Pass in Yichang, Hubei Province. The rest 65 kilometers are hills and valleys among the gorges.

Zhouyi Park, Fuling

Also known as Dianyi Cave, Zhouyi Park is located along the northern bank of the Yangtze River, facing Fuling City on the other side.

Zhouyi Park was built on the northern side of the mountain. Dianyi, the cave, was dug on the cliff. In 1095, the second year of Emperor Shaosheng's reign during the Northern Song Dynasty (960-1127), Cheng Yi, a famous idealist philosopher of Confucianism, stayed in the cave for six years, writing books and giving lectures.

The most attractive scene here is a cliff carving, 400 meters long and 20 meters high, on which there are 80 works by famous calligraphers, including Huang Tingjian, Zhu Xi, Lu You, and Wang Shizhen. On top of the cliff there is a Buddhist pagoda and several niches. There are also other attractions, including Biyun Pavilion, Gouliang Hall, Zhiyuan Pavilion, Sanwei Tower, Three-Immortal Tower, Sixian Hall, and Beiyan Academy of Classic Learning.

Traveling along the Three Gorges

Travelers usually start their journey at Chaoyangmen in Chongqing, and go downstream by boat, or take a boat at Yichang in Hubei, and go upstream. Every day there are regular pleasure boats, steamboats, and cruises, shuttling between Chongqing and Yichang, Hankou, and Shanghai.

Maple leaves in the Three Gorges.

Odd-shaped rocks in the Three Gorges.

Zhouyi Garden.

Fuling Region

Fuling is 120 kilometers from downtown Chongqing. Urban Fuling is located along the southern bank of the Yangtze River at the exit of the natural barrier of the Wujiang River. Fuling has long been famous for mustard tuber, fresh, delicious, tender, and crispy.

The new look of Fuling, a metropolis around Chongqing in the near future.

Underwater Stone Carvings

The stone carvings on the White-Crane Ridge is a relic under state protection. It is a large natural stone block located in the middle of the Yangtze River north of the Fuling District. The stone block, 1,600m by 16m, only appears on the water during the dry season. There are 164 pieces of inscriptions carved on the rock since 763, the first year during Emperor Guangde's reign of the Tang Dynasty, among which 108 are hydrological records and 14 stone fish patterns. The carved records and fish patterns present intermittently the historical dry seasons of 72 years over a span of over 1,200 years. They are of great value for the study of the regularity of dry seasons, water transportation, and production on the upper and middle reaches of the Yangtze River. At the International Hydrological Seminar held in Paris in 1974, the Chinese Delegation reported on the Inscriptions of the White-Crane Ridge in Fuling, and the value of the carvings on the stone fish has ever since been recognized by the world.

Also found on the White-Crane Ridge are poems and inscriptions by the distinguished artists and men of letters of all dynasties, hence its fame, Underwater Stone Museum.

Stone Fish on the White-Crane Ridge

The stone carvings on the stone fish are of high value for the scientific research and for the study of history and the arts. They are the historical records of the water level changes of the Yangtze. The emergence of the stone fish signifies a good harvest, as believed by the locals, which can be proven by the inscriptions on it.

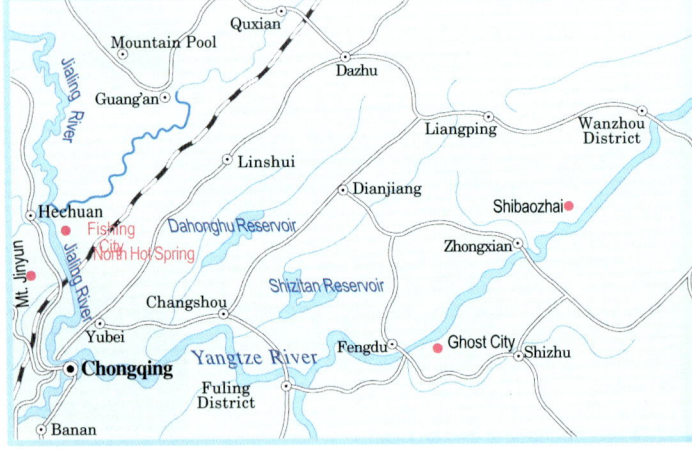

Tourist Attractions

Xiaoxi Scenic Area

The Xiaoxi Scenic Area is along the southern bank of the Wujiang River in Fuling, 14 kilometers from the city proper. There are natural wonders, such as limestone caves, ponds, waterfalls, and beautiful mountains as well as places of historic and cultural interest, such as the ruins of the ancient Ba culture. Hence its reputation of No. One Sightseeing Along the Wujiang River.

The five main tourist attractions include the Long, Secluded, Ancient Path, the Bridges over the Lake, the Limestone Cave of King Ba's Mansion, the Limestone Cave of the Mansion of Gods, and the Underground Dragon Palace. The naturally-formed three stone arch bridges of the Bridges over the Lake are the most famous among these attractions, and they span over brooks and link up two mountains. The limestone in the Underground Dragon Palace vary in shapes.

Rafting at Tiantai.

Xiaotianxi Tombs of Ba's Kings

The tombs were discovered by local farmers in April 1972 at Xiaotianxi, Chenjiazui Village of Baitao Town, 20 kilometers from Fuling City. Also brought to light were a number of important relics, including copper swords, chime bells, and animal skeletons. In late October the same year, the Sichuan and Chongqing Museums joined hands with the former Fuling Relics Group for the excavation of the tombs, unearthing 54 weapons, 41 articles for daily use, eight production tools, 37 musical instruments, and 52 other articles. All of them feature the distinctive Ba culture, coping with what was described in a local, historical record. The 14 chime bells have been displayed overseas.

Tombs of Ba's Kings

According to a historical record, "Most of the tombs of the kinds of Ba are in Fuling," which is proven by the archaeological discovery at Xiatianxi. Some 192 relics were unearthed from three tombs, and they are of high value for the study of the history and culture of the Ba people.

Shijia Gully Scenic Area

Shijia Gully is located in Longtang Village along the eastern bank of the Wujiang River, where Fuling and Wulong County meet, and touches Mt. Wuling Forest Park in the southeast. The Scenic Area mainly features karst land formation with sheer cliffs and waterfalls. It is home to 20

The Lover's Valley at Shijia Gully.

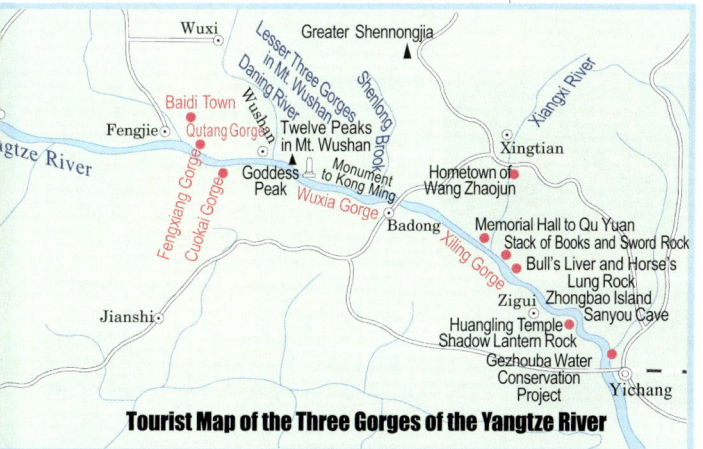

Tourist Map of the Three Gorges of the Yangtze River

The Star-and-Moon Lake in Mt. Yutai.

species of wild animals under state protection, of which the white monkey is the most precious. There are several waterfalls dropping 200 meters down and natural ground cracks, the longest of which measures 1,500 meters.

Mt. Yutai Scenic Area

It is also located along the eastern back of the Wujiang River, at an elevation of 790~870m and hemmed in by rivers and mountains, 80 percent of which is covered by plants and trees, such as pines, bamboo, and tea tree. Sanwan Lake, 803m above sea level, has an area of 46,600 square meters. On the lakeside is a garden with rich tourism resources of cultural interest, such as the Terrace to Pray for Rain and Hong'en Temple, the predecessor of Mingshan Temple in the Ghost City, Fengdu, as legend has it.

Mountains in Fengdu

The mountains in Fengdu stand along the northern bank of the Yangtze River, 172 kilometers from downtown Chongqing. It is a state Grade AAAA scenic area. During the early Western Zhou Dynasty 2,000 years ago, Fengdu served as the capital of the State of Ba and the county seat of Zhixian during the Qin and Han Dynasties. In 90, the second year of Emperor Yongyuan's reign of the Eastern Han Dynasty, it was named Pingdu due to the mountain in the east, and renamed Fengdu during the Sui Dynasty.

Origin of Mt. Mingshan

Also known as Pingdu, the mountain was so named because of a poem by Su Shi of the Song Dynasty. The saying of the Ghost in the City was originated from fairytales. Legend has it that during the Han Dynasty, two Taoists, Wang Fangping and Yin Changsheng, stayed in Mt. Pingdu, giving themselves up to austere discipline and finally achieving immortality. The mountain was soon entitled Heavenly Master.

There are 27 ancient temples on the mountain. The artists of past dynasties made thousands of Confucian and Taoist statues with clay, stone, wood, bronze, and iron, in addition to sculptures to display the court and prisons in the Nether World, to showcase the concepts of god and ghost, heaven and hell of ancient Chinese people. There are tourist attractions, such as the Temple to the Two Ferocious Gigantic Guardians, the Hall of Paying Debt of Gratitude, Mahavira Hall, the Hall of the Jade Emperor, the Hall of Hundred Children, and the Hall of the Son of Heaven. Quite a number of inscriptions and steles were written by famous men of letters, such as Su Shi, Lu You and Fan Chengda.

The Bridge over the Abyss, a passageway to hell.

Bridge over the Abyss

Erected during Emperor Yongle's reign of the Ming Dynasty, it consists of three stone arch bridges, also known as the Bridge for Immortals. The one on the left is named the Golden Bridge, and the one on the right the Silver Bridge. The one in the middle is known as the Bridge over the Abyss. The pond under the bridges is named Blood River. It is said that it is a pass to the nether world, guarded by ghosts. Good people can pass the bridge safely, and bad people will fall into the Blood River, where they will be tortured by poisonous insects and snakes. It is a warning to people that one should do things good, or he will be punished down in here without any exception.

Ghosts in the nether world.

Tourist Attractions

Palace on the Nether World

Established in 1993, the Palace on the Nether World is located 500 meters north of Fengdu County, and has a construction area of 3,000 square meters.

The Great Emperor in Fengdu.

Wangxiang Terrace in the Ghost City, Fengdu.

The Palace is a brick structure like an ancient castle surrounded by a 10m-tall, 9m-wide wall, with a huge stone sculpture of the ghost's head over the gate. In front of the gate there are two white marble sculptures of unicorn. Modern acoustic and light technologies are used to display nearly 200 stories about ghosts. Outside there is a Street of the Nether World, 200m by 24m, laid with stones. Qing-style shops line both sides of the street, with an area of 15,000 square meters.

Ghost-King Stone Carvings

The Ghost-King Stone Carvings are found on Shilinggang, nine kilometers east of Fengdu County.

Stone carvings of ghosts.

Also known as the Giant Ghost, the sculptures were carved on a rock 30,000 square meters. It is 138m by 217m, with a 20-meter mouth and 81-meter-long tongue. Completed in the 1990s, the sculptures are rough yet vivid, depicting the power of the King of Ghost with his arms holding all feelings of human beings and keeping away the evil spirits. Stone stairs lead into the body of the King of Ghost.

The Gate of Hell.

Mt. Shuanggui

Mt. Shuanggui stands in the northwestern corner of Fengdu and faces Mt. Mingshan. It has sheer cliffs and is covered by lush forest dotted by towers, terraces, and pavilions. The mountain became famous during the Tang

Choosing a ighost's headî.

Mt. Shuanggui, Fengdu.

A wet land in Fengdu.

Dynasty, when Luming Temple was built.

The Confucian Temple, the main building, is imposing with brick walls, the Nine-Dragon Wall, the Bell Tower, and the Drum Tower. The Hall of Great Achievements enshrines the statue of Confucius, accompanied by his disciples on both side. Other structures, including the Memorial Hall to Su Shi, Dongpo Tower, and Ximo Pond, were built in the early Ming Dynasty to commemorate Su Shi, a literary giant in Chinese history.

Rafting Along the Dragon River

The Dragon River, 140 kilometers long, descends from Mt. Wulong and joins the Yangtze River at Xincheng, Fengdu. The landscapes along the banks are beautiful, and the gorges are dangerously steep. Maliang Bridge is the starting point for drafting, which can last for 12 kilometers, with five gorges and 30 shoals. The gorges are green and secluded, and the shoals have rushing waters and high waves.

Shibaozhai

Shibaozhai.

Shibaozhai, or Shibao Village, is located along the northern bank of the Yangtze in Zhongxian County, 38 kilometers from the ancient township of Zhongzhou. A sheer, huge rock rises over 30 meters above the ground. The village used to be where the Tanhong Uprising started in the late Ming Dynasty. Hence its name.

The Village was built by Mt. Yuyin in a precipitous way. The main building has double eaves and looks grandeur. The village consists of three parts, the gate, the village, and the wooden-structured watchtower with 12 stories measuring 56 meters high. The stairs within the Tower is the only way leading to the village top. There are three groups of sculptures in the village. One tells the story of General Manzi of the Ba, who killed himself to protect the village; another depicts the scene of General Zhang Fei of the legendary Three Kingdoms, who set his captive Yan Yan free to make the latter join his troops; and the one about heroine Qin Liangyu.

Liu Bei, king of the State of Shu, was badly ill after being defeated in his war declared against the State of Eastern Wu. Just before his death he asked Zhuge Liang, his prime minister, to take care of his son at the Palace of Everlasting Peace in Baidi Town.

Shibaozhai was first built during the reign of Emperor Wanli of the Ming Dynasty and was reconstructed during the reigns of Emperors Kangxi and Qianlong of the Qing Dynasty. It was formerly a nine-story structure, symbolizing the highest of heavens. Another three stories were added to the building in 1956 while the village was restored. Today, Shibaozhai is a relic under major state protection.

Ladder Street at Xituo

Xituo Town of the Shizhu Tu Autonomous County faces Shibaozhai on the other side of the river. It is located on the slope along the riverside of the Yangtze, led by a 2,500-meter-long stairs, 1,124 in total. Looking from the Yangtze, the stairs resemble a ladder up to the sky. Hence its name.

A street in Xituo

Tourist Attractions

The ancient township of Xituo used to be a busy ferry as early as the Han Dynasty, a distribution center for local products in Sichuan and Hubei Provinces. It is featured by compound houses and houses made of timber and bamboo and supported by wooden stakes over ground, along the hillside.

Temple to General Zhang Fei

Located at the foot of Mt. Feifeng along the southern bank of the Yangtze River, the Temple is 382 kilometers from downtown Chongqing and faces Yunyang County on the other side of the river. It was built to commemorate Zhang Fei, a distinguished general of the Three Kingdoms Period. According to historical records, it was first built in the late kingdom period of Shu Han (221~263), one of the Three Kingdoms, and was reconstructed during the Song, Yuan, Ming, and Qing Dynasties (960~1911).

The Temple stands on a huge rock along the riverside. On the cliff in front of the Temple there are four Chinese characters, "江上清风". Entering the Temple, one can see the tall, solemn Jieyi Tower, or the Tower Where They (Liu Bei, Guan Yu, and Zhang Fei) Become Sworn Brothers. In the middle of the main hall stands a large statue of General Zhang Fei, accompanied by two sculptures of warrior horses. The Tower of Watching the Cloud is secluded and elegant.

The Temple has a collection of 600 poems, calligraphy, paintings, and steles, as well as more than 1,000 relics, among which the wooden carvings of calligraphy by Yan Zhenqing, the stone carvings of the poems by Su Shi, the stone carvings by Yue Fei, the poems inscribed by Huang Tingjian, and the poems and paintings by Zheng Banqiao are the most precious. It is reputed as a Holly Land for the Works by Literary Giants.

The Temple was removed in July 2003 to another site, more than 10 kilometers up the reaches of the Yangtze due to the construction of the Three Gorges Project. The resettled Temple remains as what it looked like before with the exact environment, and it was rebuilt with the original bricks and tiles. The only difference is the expansion of the exhibition hall.

Temples to Zhang Fei and Du Fu

The Temple to General Zhang Fei was built according to the terrain of the mountain and faces the river. It is a magnificent building complex, and consists of seven structures, such as the Main Hall, the Wing Hall, Jieyi Tower, or the Tower Where They (Liu Bei, Guan Yu, and Zhang Fei) Become Sworn Brothers, the Tower of Watching the Cloud, Zhufeng Tower, and the pavilions of Azaleas and Deyue. The last two structures were built to commemorate Du Fu, a distinguished poet of the Tang Dynasty.

The Western Chamber of Du Fu, where he wrote 380 poems.

The Phoenix Tablet.

The Pavilion to Observe the Stars.

Ancient Town of Panshi

Located in the new county seat of Yunyang, the ancient township of Panshi resembles a stone mill, hence its nickname Stone Mill Village. It is surrounded by sheer cliffs on all sides, and rests on a huge, natural rock, where the Yangtze and the Pengxi River meet. First built in the Southern Song Dynasty, it covers an area of 35,000 square meters, at an elevation of 100 meters. There are front and rear gates and other defensive facilities, such as watchtowers and observation towers, two forts, one in the north and another in the south, weapon and ammunition depots, grain storage, and catch basins. The geographical location made the township a place of military importance over the dynasties.

More than 80 steles of the Sui and Qing Dynasties are displayed in the Eastern and Western Stele Forest.

The White Dragon in the legend, which gave inspiration for Gongsun Shu to name the township as Baidi.

Baidi Temple.

Baidi Town

Baidi Town, known as Ziyang, is located along the northern bank of the Yangtze River, 451 kilometers from downtown Chongqing. It is said that in the late Western Han Dynasty, Gongsun Shu occupied the area and called himself the King of Shu. One day he saw the white smoke rising from a local well in the form of a white dragon, and thus decided to establish his capital here by renaming it as Baidi Town (White Emperor City), and call himself Emperor Baidi. The site we see today is the ruins restored during the Ming and Qing Dynasties.

Baidi Town was a strategic military pass because it is surrounded by water on three sides, and situated by Kuimen in the east and by the Eight Battle-Formation Diagram in the west.

Tourist Attractions

Baidi Town is the best place for watching the magnificent Kuimen. Many poets, such as Li Bai, Du Fu, Bai Juyi, Liu Yuxi, Su Shi, Huang Tingjian, Fan Chengda, and Lu You, found inspiration here for their poems. So the city got its alias as the City of Poems. Today, Baidi is a state Grade AAAA scenic area.

Baidi Temple

In the Three Kingdoms Period, Liu Bei, king of the State of Shu, was badly ill after being defeated in his war declared against the State of Eastern Wu. Just before his death he asked Zhuge Liang, his prime minister, to take care of his son at the Palace of Everlasting Peace in Baidi Town. Clay figurines about this story are on display in the Baidi Temple.

Some relics discovered from the suspended coffin in the Qutang Gorge, 73 pieces of steles, over 1,000 relics of the past dynasties, and more than 100 calligraphy and paintings are also exhibited in the temple.

The Iron Lock Pass

At the foot of the precipice and on the steep rocks of Kuimen, two large iron pillars stand to split the rushing Yangtze River. The pillars, two meters tall, are connected by seven iron chains, 90 meters long.

Eight Battle-Formation Diagram

It is located along the northern bank of the Yangtze River, 1,000 meters east of Fengjie County. A little river runs through the beach stretching into the river, which is 1,500 meters long and over 600 meters wide. It is said that Zhuge Liang, prime minister of the State of Shu, had designed the Eight Battle-Formation Diagram here while entering Sichuan Province. He ordered his men to construct the formation by stocking stones. There are all together 64 battlements in the formation by placing them 8 by 8. In addition, another 24 battlements garrisoning patrols were set on the outskirts of the formation. Each battlement is five inches high and six inches wide by spacing nine inches from one another.

According to *Romance of Three Kingdoms*, General Lu Xun of the State of Wu led his army following up the defeated Shu troops westwards. The Wu troops ran into the Eight Battle-Formation Diagram laid by Zhuge Liang and were nearly ambushed while getting confused and losing the sense of direction inside the formation. Finally the Wu army had no choice but to retreat to their own territories.

Eight Battle-Formation Diagram

It was here that Du Fu found inspiration for his poems.

Chijia Tower at the Qutang Gorge.

A bird's-eye view of Baidi.

Qutang Gorge

Also known as Kuimen, the Qutang Gorge starts from Baidi Town, Fengjie in the west and ends at Dixi, Wushan in the east. The Qutang Gorge is particularly famous for its grandeur among the Three Gorges. The rocks on both sides of the access to the gorge are as precipitous as being cut by knives and axes. The water roars through the space as narrow as only 100 meters.

Qutang Gorge is noted for its great scenery of Qutang Inscription Steep Rocks, the Mengliang Ladder, the Phoenix Spring, and the Peak of a Rhinoceros Watching the Moon on the southern bank, in addition to the fantastic scenery, such as the Seven Gates, the Wind Boxes Gorge, and the Qutang Plank Road on the northern bank. Among the Qutang Inscription Steep Rocks are some important inscriptions singing high praise for Kuimen.

There is a man-made plank road on the high and steep precipice along the northern bank of the Yangtze River. Situated between the cliff peaks and rushing water, the plank road served as the sole means of military transportation, track road and business path in ancient times. Eight Chinese characters were engraved on the rock beside the road. The valley named Seven Gates, as deep as over 100 meters, lie right beside the Plank Road. A skylight faces the river between the rocks from where one can look upward to enjoy the two peaks and blue sky, and downward to watch the boats sailing on the rapids of the river. Looking into the caves one may find two groups of vivid stalactites in the form of animals and birds.

A couple of wooden boxes were put between the rocks which are nearly 100 meters high. The wooden boxes are in the shape of bellows, hence their name Bellow Gorge. The boxes are said to belong to the famous carpenter Lu Ban, and they are precisely hung as coffins.

Wuxia Gorge

Beginning from the Daning River in Wushan County in the west and ending at the Guandu Pass in Badong County, Hubei Province, the zigzagging Wuxia Gorge is a picturesque art gallery abundant with beautiful mist and mountain scenery.

The scenic spots in the Wuxia Gorge are the three platforms including the Chuyang Platform, the Shoushu Platform, and the Zhanlong Platform, in addition to eight wonders such as the Nanling Spring Dawn on the Top of Mt. Nanling, the Setting Sun in Yangliuping, Fishing in the Qingxi River,

Stone carvings on the sheer cliff.

The ancient plank road at Qutang Gorge starts from Baidi Town and ends at Qinglian Brook in Mt. Wushan, 65 kilometers long. It was completed during the reign of Emperor Guangxu of the Qing Dynasty.

The cloud-capped Mt. Wushan.

Wuxia Gorge takes pride in its 12 peaks.

Chongtan Autumn Moon over the Ninghe River, Xiufeng Buddhist Temple on Mt. Wufeng, the Rock of Wife Watching Her Husband south of the city, and the Cloud in the Morning and Rain at Night. Wuxia is also famous for its twelve peaks, including Denglong, Shengquan, Zhaoyun, Shennu (Goddess), Songluan, Jixian, Feifeng, Cuiping, Juhe, Jingtan, Qiyun, and Shangsheng.

Goddess Peak

The Goddess Peak is the most famous among the twelve peaks. A stone pillar looking like a slim girl stands atop the peak, and she is the first one who welcomes the sun and sees her off. According to a book written by Tang Guangcheng, Yao Ji, the youngest daughter of the Queen Mother of the West, traveled around the East China Sea and Mt. Wushan, and they ran into the flood. She saw the ending of the flood and stood on the peak for so long that she finally turned out to be part of the Goddess Peak so as to pray for good harvests and safe sailing.

Xiling Gorge

Beginning from Xiangxikou in the west and ending at the Nanjin Pass in the east, the Xiling Gorge is famous for its winding waterway, numerous dangerous shoals, jagged rocks, and rapids. Transportation has been guaranteed since the construction of the Three Gorges Water Conservation Project in June 2003.

Sailing out of the Nanjin Pass declares the ending of the 300-*li* journey of the Xiling Gorge. The Yangtze River starts its middle reaches from here. The river becomes abruptly broader, and thousands of hectares of farmlands lie along the banks.

The Peak of Goddess.

Xiling Gorge in spring.

Princess Wang Zhaojun

According to the *Chronicles of the Han Dynasty*, Princess Wang Zhaojun married the king of Xiongnu, or Hun, ancient nomadic people living in North China, in 33 B.C. The marriage enhanced the friendship as well as cultural and economic relationship between the peoples of Han and Xiongnu, and the princess was highly praised by later generations. There are many legends and relics about Wang Zhaojun, such as the Stockade Village of Zhaojun, the Feitai Hill, and the Platform of Zhaojun.

The hometown of Princess Wang Zhaojun.

Qu Yuan
(C.340~277B.C.)

Qu Yuan, a great statesman and patriotic poet in China, served as minister of the State of Chu in the late Warring States Period. Upon hearing that the capital of the State of Chu was captured by the Qin army, Qu Yuan threw himself into the Miluo River in Hunan Province to show his faith to his country. In 1953, the World Peace Council cited him as one of the four Cultural Celebrities of the World.

Hometown of Qu Yuan

The Hometown of Qu Yuan near the new district of Zigui County, more than 500 kilometers from Chongqing, was rebuilt after the construction of the Three Gorges Project.

In the Hometown of Qu Yuan there is a temple to commemorate Qu Yuan, minister of the State of Chu and one of China's earliest poets. Over the imposing gate of the Temple there are three Chinese characters inscribed by Guo Moruo.

A bronze statue of Qu Yuan stands right in the middle of the courtyard, three tons in weight and 3.92 meters in height, on a 2.5-meter-tall base. Ninety stone steles are found on both sides of the bronze statue, with inscriptions of 22 poems by Qu Yuan, as well as poems praising Qu Yuan by distinguished poets, including Li Bai and Du Fu, and records on the construction of the Temple and the Tomb of Qu Yuan.

Various editions of *The Poetry of Chu* and the footnotes are stored in Memorial Hall. A stone statue of Qu Yuan, 250 kg, carved in 1537 with donations from the local people, stands in the Hall. It is the first of its kind in China.

The tomb of Qu Yuan covers an area of 120 square meters, and is a fan-shape complex with three rows and six pillars. A red coffin of Qu Yuan is suspended over the access to the tomb.

Xiangxi Brook

Xiangxi Brook is at the entrance of the Xiling Gorge along the northern bank of the Yangtze River, 572 kilometers from downtown Chongqing.

The beautiful Xiangxi descends from Mt. Shennongjia, runs through the cracks of limestone, and is filtered and precipitated by caves. The crystal-clear water flows southwards and finally empties itself into the Yangtze.

It would be a great pleasure watching the Peach Blossom Fish in Xiangxi. In the early spring, a kind of coelenterate in the shape of jellyfish appear in the river. Just because they are quite similar to the peach blossoms both in shape and color, the name of Peach Blossom was gifted to them by local people.

Xiangxi is attractive with oranges growing on both sides of the brook and rolling hills.

The Three Gorges Project

December 1994 saw the construction of the Three Gorges Project at Sandouping, the upper section of the Xiling Gorge

Xiling Gorge in the setting sun.

Tourist Attractions

on the Yangtze River, which was cut in November 1997. The Project will last for two decades and costs a total of 90.09 billion yuan. Some 1.1318 million people will resettle because of the Project.

The dam is 185 meters above sea level, and spans over 2,300 meters. The initial processing water level in 2006 will reach 165 meters high, and the final processing water level in 2009, 175 meters high. The water level came to 135 meters above sea level in June 2003, when the two-way and five-scale ship lock was adopted. The reservoir covers an area of 1,084 square kilometers, with a storage of 39.3 billion cubic meters and an anti-flood storage of 22.15 billion cubic meters. The total installed hydroelectric capacity is 17.68 million kw, and the annual generating capacity is 84 billion kwh. The first generating plant was put into operation in 2003.

The ship locks of the Three Gorges Project open to traffic.

The Three Gorges Project, China's largest water conservation project, will play an important part in anti-flood, power generation, navigation, water conservation, and tourism.

Gezhouba Water Conservation Project

Situated at the end of the Xiling Gorge, Gezhouba was constructed in 1974 and completed in 1988. It used to be China's largest water conservation project prior to the Three Gorges Project.

Gezhouba is 2,595 meters long, 70 meters tall, and 30 meters wide. It consists of the power station, the ship locks, the sluice gates, and the scouring sluice. It has a total storage capacity of 158,000 cubic meters, and controls a drainage area of one million square kilometers. The power station has 21 generators with an annual generation capacity of 14.1 billion kwh, three ship locks, large enough to handle 10,000-ton ships. The 27 sluice gates and 15 scouring sluices have a maximum flood discharging capacity of 110,000 cubic meters per second.

Xiling Yangtze River Bridge

The highway bridge was erected at the Xiling Gorge for the construction of the Three Gorges Project. It is 1,118.66 meters long, 18 meters wide, and 30 meters tall above the river. The cable tower is 187.5 meters tall and spans 900 meters, and has a handling capacity of 4,770 tons.

Tourist Attractions

Lesser Three Gorges Tourist Area, Wushan

The Lesser Three Gorges Tour Area of Mt. Wushan mainly consists of the Daning River and its surrounding areas. Major tourist attractions include the Lesser Three Gorges, the Small Lesser Three Gorges of the Madu River, the Ancient Town of Dachang, the Cultural Ruins at Daxi, and the Ancient Ape-Man Site at Longgupo.

Lesser Three Gorges, Daning River

Also known as Changhe and Wuxi, the Daning River descends from the southern foot of Mt. Daba and empties itself into the Yangtze River at the western exit of the Wuxia Gorge. Running 250 kilometers long, it is the largest tributary at the Three Gorges section of the Yangtze.

The Lesser Three Gorges is referred to the three gorges, including Longmen, Bawu, and Dicui on the lower reaches of the Daning River. It starts from Longmen in the south and ends at Tujiaba in the north, with a total length of 50 kilometers. People can enjoy the magnificent view of mountains, peaks, perilous shoals, crystal clear water, grotesque stones, and secluded scenes. This place has been cited as one of China's Top 40 Tourist Attractions.

Longmen, or the Dragon Gate, starts from the mouth of the Ninghe River, and ends at Dongpingba, three kilometers in length. This gorge is as magnificent as the Qutang Gorge, and is more like Kuimen. There are scenic spots, such as the Longmen Bridge, the ancient plank road, the Lion Guard of the Gate, the Nine-Dragon Pillar, and Pipa Islet.

Bawu, or the Mist Gorge, starts from Dongpingba and ends at Shuanglong Town, 10 kilometers in length. The mountains are high and valleys deep. The grotesque rocks form a natural picture. Major tourist attractions include Mt. Magui, the Suspended Coffins, and Shuanglong Town.

Dicui, or the Emerald Gorge, starts from Shuanglong Town and ends at Tujiaba, 20 kilometers in length. Along the gorge there are precipices and peaks rising one after another. It is the most secluded, beautiful and poetic among the Lesser Three Gorges, with a number of scenic spots, such as the Ox Losing its Tail, the Water Curtain Cave, Broadleaf Plants, Ox's Liver and Horse's Lung, cliff carvings of Buddhist statues, Heaven Spring with Flying Rain, Luojia Village, Sheep Cliff, Madu River, Heaven Peak, Golden Monkey Peak, Red Cliff, Boat Coffin, Two Eagles Playing in the Screen, Flying-Cloud Cave, and Guest-Greeting Spring.

A girl by the river of Ninghe.

From Chongqing to the Lesser Three Gorges in Mt. Wushan Transportation in the Tourist Area

It will be a pleasant trip if one takes a boat at Chaotianmen to Mt. Wushan. One can also take a bus at Caiyuanba.

Nine Dams & 13 Gorges

The highlights of the Wujiang River include nine dams and 13 gorges. The nine dams include Baitao, Baima, Xiangkou, Jiangkou, Tieqiba, Luojiatuo, Sandongqi, Wanzu, and Hongdu. The 13 gorges are Sanmen, Biantan, Yanjing, Piao'er, Zhongzui, Xianshan, Luju, Menshuan, Luojiatuo, Mozhai, Mafengyan, Longmen and Banbian.

The Lesser Three Gorges in the early morning.

Dicui Gorge.

Chongqing Tourist Guide

Lesser Three Gorges, Daning River

Tourists can enjoy the sightseeing by boat upstream from the ferry at Mt. Wushan, get off halfway, and enjoy the rest trip by collecting pebbles, taking photos, playing with water, and have picnic along the banks.

The plank road and the cable bridge in the Lesser Three Gorges.

Water-Curtain Cave

It is not far from the entrance to the Dicui Gorge. On the cliff along the western bank there is a deep limestone cave, where clear spring water flow slowly down to a stalactite, forming a water curtain above the river.

A watching Terrace for Suspended Coffins was built on the other side of the river, where people can see the suspended coffins at the Bawu Gorge with telescopes.

Cliff coffins of the Han Dynasty at the Jingzhu Gorge, Wuxi.

Lion Guard of the Gate

Along the western bank of Longmen stands a peak in the shape of a lion among the bush, guarding the Dragon Gate day and night. Hence its name.

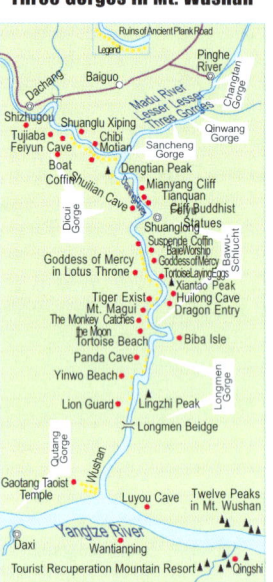

Ancient Plank Road at Ninghe

The site of ancient plank road is found on the cliffs of the western side of Longmen, 15 meters from the river. There are numerous regular and square stone caves arranged in order, 20 centimeters in diameter and 30 centimeters deep. They are distributed like the upside down Chinese character "品". Based on this form, a triangle prop-up was set up to spread plates on the upper two wooden piles, with another pile being inserted on the low hole propping up the wooden plate. The plank road was constructed for the local people and their transportation of life stocks.

The ancient plank road along the bank of the Ninghe River links up Longmen, Wuxi County, Zhenping County in Shaanxi Province, Xixian County in Hubei Province, and Chengkou County in Chongqing. Stretching 400 kilometers long, it is the longest ancient plank road in China.

Suspended Coffin

On a tawny cliff along the eastern bank of the Mist Gorge, about 400 to 500 meters high, there is a rectangular cave with a black wooden coffin inside. It is known as the Suspended Coffin, a custom of the Pu people inhabiting the Daning River region some 2,000 years ago to bury a dead person, whereby the coffin was placed in a cave or crevice in a cliff. According to historical records of Tang Dynasty, the Pus sold all their valuable stuff for a coffin for their parents. They buried the coffin in a drilled hole half way of high mountains nearby the river and suspended it from the mountain top. It was believed that the higher the coffin was suspended, the more they were believed to be in mourning.

Tourist Map of the Lesser Three Gorges in Mt. Wushan

Tourist Attractions

Boat Coffins

A black wooden boat is found to be placed on a 200-meter-high inclined terrace on the western bank of the Emerald Gorge, which is known as boat coffin, another custom to bury the dead person of the ancient Bas. The custom was probably originated from the fishermen in the Daning River region.

The Emerald Gorge's boat coffin seems to be very grotesque. What's more grotesque is its surrounding natural environment. Ten meters away from the left of the boat coffin is a sheaf of black old rattan spreading out from the cliff crevices, which resemble fishing net. About 50 meters to the left is a 5-meter-high stalactite, which looks like an old man wearing a straw hat, bending over to extend his fishing net. In his hands, there is a tree root extending into the river like a fishnet's rope. Here are the Boat, the Fishing Net, and the Fisherman, making up a Fishing Village.

Cliff coffins in Shizhu County.

Small Lesser Three Gorges

The Madu River, a tributary of the Ninghe River on the eastern bank of the Emerald Gorge, descends from the depth of Mt. Daba, flows southwestward, and joins the Daning River near Dengtian Peak. The Small Lesser Three Gorges refers to the three gorges, including Sancheng, Qinwang, and Changtan, each of which measures five kilometers in length.

Sancheng, or Three Poles, is a narrow gorge with sheer cliffs and violent current. Since there is no towing path along the gorge, it is impossible to sail upstream if not using poles to constantly push the boat. Hence the name of the gorge.

There is a big limestone cave on the eastern bank of the Qinwang, or the King of Qin, Gorge. It is said that there was a man named Qin, who supervised to make explosives with the instruction of the emperor. He was made the king for

Rafting safely along the Small Lesser Three Gorges.

The Small Lesser Three Gorges.

Playing with water in the Lesser Three Gorges.

Transportation of the Small Lesser Three Gorges Tourist Area

The Small Lesser Three Gorges of the Madu River is connected with the Lesser Three Gorges of the Daning River. It might be a good idea to travel by boat. Take a boat to Madukou, shift a little wooden boat upstream, and get off at the last stop. Those who are interested in rafting can take rubber dinghy, rafting downstream.

his excellent service. Hence the name of the cave and the Gorge.

The name of the Changtan, or Long Shoal, Gorge was given because of a 2,000-meter-long shoal, narrow and straight, and sandwiched by magnificent and perilous precipices facing each other. The water is so clear that one can see fish of various species playing in the river. On the beach there are colorful pebbles, apparently fossils of ancient living creatures.

The ancient town of Dachang.

An old house.

Ancient Town of Dachang

Dachang, 10 kilometers north of the Emerald Gorge, was first established in the Jin Dynasty some 1,700 years ago. As the largest township along the Ninghe River, it used to be a county seat for the past dynasties. Three city gates in the east, south and west are well preserved. There are also several well-preserved streets built during the Ming and Qing Dynasties. Walking along the street, one can see old-fashioned archways and architectures with engraved beams, painted pillars, and upturned eaves. This area will be submerged during the construction of the second phase of the Three Gorges Project, and major structures will be moved to the new site of Dachang.

Lu You Cave

Located at the juncture of the Wuxia Gorge and the Daning

Weaving up his life: An old man in Shizhu.

Tourist Attractions

River, 2,500 meters from Wushan County, Lu You Cave consists of three ancient caves, including Qingshui, Jinzhu, and Yulin, which are independent but connected. Stalactites in the caves are varied in gestures, some resembling lying rhinoceros, others like jade pillars. In 1170, the sixth year of Emperor Xiaozong's reign of the Song Dynasty, Lu You, a distinguished poet, visited the cave and stayed overnight. Hence the name.

Cultural Ruins at Daxi

Located at the converge of the eastern narrows of the Qutang Gorge and the Daxi Brook, 15 kilometers from Fengjie County, the Cultural Ruins, 570 square meters in area, was excavated in 1958, 1975 and 1976, and 1,200 relics were brought to light from 208 tombs, including production tools, ornaments, and arts and crafts. The culture has been proven to be 5,000 or 6,000 years old, dating back to the late period of the matriarchal society or the early stage of the patriarchal society. It is one of the famous ruins of ancient Chinese culture, and of high value for the study of the New Stone Age as well as the social and economic development of the upper reaches of the Yangtze River.

Daxi Cultural Ruins in Wushan County.

Ancient Ape-Man Site at Longgupo

Located at Longgupo of Longping Village, Miaoyu Town in Wushan County, the Site covers an area of 700 square meters. It was excavated in 1986, when fossils of ancient human front teeth and jaw bones with canine teeth were unearthed, along with dozens of fossils of giant monkeys, saber-toothed tigers and twin-angler rhinoceros. Textual researches prove that these fossils are some 2.04 million years old. This discovery has filled in the gaps of early human fossils in China, contributing remarkably to the study of human origins and the history of the development of the

Jinzhu Cave

Above Qingshui (Clear Water) Cave is Jinzhu (Golden Bamboo) Cave. The two caves are connected by 200-odd steps. Looking down from Jinzhu, one can see the reflection of the 24-section, leaf-shaped colorful lanterns in the depth of the pond. Outside Jinzhu are structures built after the model of ancient buildings, where people can admire the Wuxia Gorge in the distance.

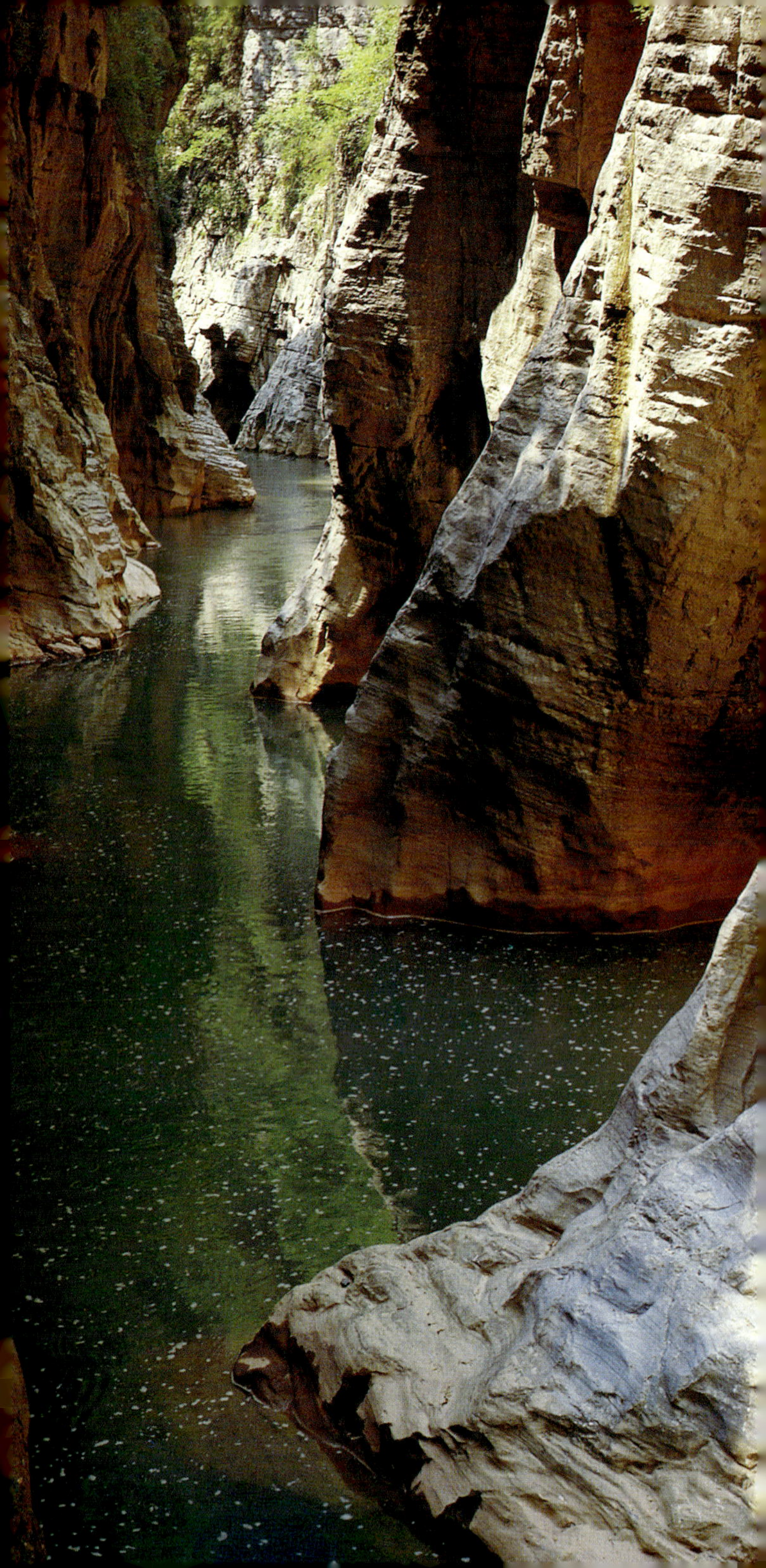

three-river valleys.

Three Gorges' Hinterland Scientific Exploration Tourist Area

The Hinterland Scientific Exploration Tourist Area in the Three Gorges area consists of the Wanzhou District and the counties of Fengjie, Yunyang, and Wuxi. Tourist programs include scientific investigation and adventurous tour. It features natural pits, ground cracks, the Dragon Jar, Hongchiba, the Summer Ice Cave, and the Han Tombs at Tujing.

Taibai Rock

Located in Mt. Xishan, Wanzhou, Taibai Rock towers 173 meters high, stretches for three kilometers long, and covers an area of 600,000 square meters. It used to be a famous mountain in the Wei and Jin Dynasties and give inspiration for many noted poets, such as Li Bai, Huang Tingjian, Lu You, and He Qifang. In the mid 1980s, a park named Taibai was built halfway up the mountain. Today, it is a famous scenic spot with natural landscapes and places of cultural and historic interest in the Three Gorges area. It is also a sacred place for Confucianism, Taoism, and Buddhism.

Shennu (Goddess) Brook.

Qinglong Waterfall

Located along the banks of the Ganning River in the Wanzhou District, 34 kilometers from the city proper, Qinglong Waterfall is 105 meters wide and 64.5 meters tall. All year round, it drops with a great thunder, which can be heard miles away, into a 25-meter-deep pool, known as the Black Dragon, forming rainbows in the sunlight.

The Black Dragon Waterfall in Wanzhou.

Han Tombs at Xujing

The Han Tombs are located at Hongchi Village of Tujing Township, 25 kilometers northeast of Zhongxian County, and consist of 15 tombs.

Along the path in the cave, there is a terra-cotta horse drawing a cart by a well. There are various kinds of terra-cotta figurines, silver, bronze, and iron articles and decorations.

Among the tombs, the best preserved is No. 5 of the Three Kingdoms Period, in which are displayed relics in order. The burial articles are mainly terra-cotta figurines and wares made during the Three Kingdoms Period.

Han Watchtowers

Transportation Between Chongqing and Wanzhou

Both boats and long-distance buses are available for traveling between Chongqing and Wanzhou District. Most buses can take visitors to scenic spots in Wanzhou and its surrounding areas.

Wanzhou District, a gateway to eastern Chongqing.

Tianzi City, Wanzhou District

With towering peaks and steep cliffs, it is an ancient village with only one access to the village—the gate. Also known as Tiansheng, it is said to be the place where Liu Bei stationed his troops when he prepared to invade the State of Wu. It is one of the Eight Scenic Wonders in Wanzhou.

Ancestral Temple to Bai Juyi

Located in the Western Hill Park in Zhongxian County, the Temple was built to commemorate Bai Juyi, a great poet of the Tang Dynasty, who served as regional chief of Zhongzhou, today's Zhongxian. First built in 1630, the third year of Emperor Chongzhen's reign during the Ming Dynasty, and reconstructed in later years, it enshrines a stone statue of Bai Juyi and showcased the stone slab used by Bai and other precious relics.

Map of Scenic Spots in Fengjie

Watchtowers are a stone structure, in pairs, six meters high, standing symmetrically on either side of a palace gate. They were mostly erected in the Han Dynasty. Hence its name. They were symbolic structures of nobility and dignity. There are only 30 pairs in China, three of which are found in Zhongxian. They are of high value for the study of the architecture of the Han Dynasty.

Non-inscription Watchtowers

Also known as pagoda, it is located in Youxi Village, Tujing Town, eight kilometers north of Zhongxian County. Built in the Eastern Han Dynasty yet well preserved, it is 5.44 meters high, eight by eight meters, and has nine stories. Built with nine blocks of stones in different shapes, the structure is mutually connected and piled up. The base is thick, strong, and steady. A dragon-and-tiger-like animal was carved on the body, and a strong, naked male and a female were carved respectively on the sides of the third and sixth floors, brave, vigorous, and handsome. Bending their backs with their kneels down in full strength, the figures seem to carry the entire structure. Birds and animals were engraved around the figures.

Dingfang Twin Watchtowers

The Twin Watchtowers are located in front of Bawang Temple outside the eastern gate of Zhongxian. Built during the late Eastern Han Dynasty, they are the best of their kind in China. Virtually temple watchtowers, they are seven

Dingfang Twin Watchtowers.

Tourist Attractions

meters high, and stand two meters aside, one in the east, another in the west. The roof has double eaves laid with double-layered stones, with relief on all sides. The watchtowers were engraved with odd birds and animals, figures and tales, auspicious clouds, and symmetrical patterns. On top of the palatial roof, there are also vividly depicted patterns.

Temple of Twin Osmanthus

Located in Shuanggui (Twin Osmanthus) Village, 13 kilometers southwest of Liangping County, the Temple was built in 1653, the 10th year of Emperor Shunzhi's reign during the Qing Dynasty.

The Temple, 70,000 square meters in area, is a wooden and stone structure well furnished for Buddhist activities. All works of art, including stone steles, wooden carvings, calligraphy, and paintings, were exquisitely made. It consists of the Front Gate, the Maitreya Hall, the Mahavira Hall, the Hall of Disciplines, Poshan Pagoda, Hall of Great Mercy, and the Tripitaka Pavilion. Unique in design, the imposing Temple has 328 wing rooms connected with long corridors. There are a great number of painted and clay figurines, and brick, stone, and wooden carvings. In recent years, 500 figurines of arhats have been made, exquisite and vivid.

The Han Watchtower.

The Temple of Twin Osmanthus is a famous sacred place for Buddhism as well as a well-known tourist attraction in China. There are man-made rock-eries, gardens, and secluded, beautiful environments with plants and streams.

Dragon Jar

Located at Qingshui, 80 kilometers from Yunyang County, the Dragon Jar is the largest vertical, limestone well in the world. It looks like a round, natural pit in the shape of water jar. The wall is covered by Chinese wisteria and decorated with wild flowers. The lower part of the wall in dark grey is sharp. Throwing stones into the pit, it takes some time to hear the echo. There seems to be small animals running inside, and birds named Flying Tiger wheel in and out of the pit, with its wings as sharp as knives. It is said that there used to be a man tying himself halfway the wall with thick hemp rope. He was attacked by a Flying Tiger. The rope was broken, the man fell into the wall, and died. On the southern edge of the jar there is a 5-meter-high huge rock, on top of which lies a 2-meter-long rectangular stone slab.

Qixia Palace

Also known as Yunsheng, the Palace is located five kilometers northwest of Yunyang County. First built in the Han Dynasty and constantly repaired during the Southern

Relics in Shuanggui Hall

The Shuanggui Hall has a rich collection of relics, including musical instruments bestowed by Emperor Yongzheng of the Qing Dynasty, a Tripitaka, a stone tablet of the imperial edict, a Buddhist Scriptures on Pattra in Sanskrit, 7,000 volumes of Buddhist scriptures, 12 volumes of Quotations, and calligraphy in the running-hand.

A waterfall in Wuxi.

The Origin of Hongchiba

In ancient times, this area was a lake called Wanqingchi, or Hongchi. As water ran out, the lake became an alpine silted-up plain, 40 kilometers long from east to west and seven kilometers wide from north to south. The Red (Hong in Chinese) Army used to stay here. Hence its name.

Summer Ice Cave

In the Cave, one can see a wonderful view of melting ice in the spring and freezing ice in thre summer. The most impressive scene are the "ice waterfalls" on the walls: some like surging rivers about to breach, others like floods rushing down the cliffs, or like roaring waterfalls.

The alpine pastureland at Hongchiba.

and Northern Dynasties, the imposing structure is one of the famous places for Taoism in the country. The Palace, built on mountain top and surrounded by green pines, has rising eaves, painted beams, and engraved pillars. The big, tall columns are based on decorations of vivid tigers and leopards. There are statues sitting in the Palace. In front of the main hall there is a big oven for making pills of immorality. Couplets and poems are hung on the pillars. It is said that Fujia of the Han Dynasty once lived here in seclusion for fear of Qin's unrest, and planted an arhat pine when leaving, and the tree can still be seen here.

Hongchiba Alpine Pastureland Forest Park

Located along the northern bank of the Yangtze River, 80 kilometers northwest of Wuxi County, the Forest Park covers an area of 280,000 *mu,* at an elevation of 1,800 to 2500 meters. It features a karst land formation. There are scenic spots, such as Mt. Azaleas, Tianzi City, Yinguang Terrain, Zhalupan, Xiliu Brook, and the Summer Ice Cave. At the bottom of the valley, there are terrains, wide and flat, with pleasant summer, thus making it an ideal summer resort. The temperature in winter is as low as 23°C, and the three-month frozen period makes the place an ideal choice for skiing and skating.

Summer Ice Cave

The Summer Ice Cave is in the Hongchiba Alpine Pastureland Forest Park on the upper reaches of the Daning River, 80 kilometers west of Wuxi County. The entrance of the Cave, 2,200 meters above sea level, faces east, in a shape of triangle. It is three meters high, five meters wide, and 10 meters long. In the summer, there are trees and azaleas outside the Cave; while inside, it is a world of ice. Hence its name.

The ground crack in Tianjing Gorge.

Tourist Attractions

Ground Crack

It is located in the Xinglong District, 91 kilometers from Fengjie County. A natural crevice can be seen on the ground between two parallel mountains with lush trees and filled with mist.

The crevice is 80~200 meters deep and 14 kilometers long, and its bottom measures three~30 meters wide. It consists of two sections, the upper and the lower. The upper section ranges from the Big Elephant Hill to Chigucao, eight kilometers in length. A 3.5-kilometer-long path from the Tianjing Gorge leads down to the bottom. The cliffs on both sides are as precipitous as cut by a knife. At the bottom there is a waterfall cave, and water flows after the rain. The lower section consists of a natural pit and the Labyrinth Gorge. It has been proven to be a six-kilometer-long hidden cave by British adventurers in August 1994.

The underground river in the Tianjing Gorge.

Natural Pit at Xiaozhai

The Natural Pit, geologically known as karst funnel landform, is located in Xiaozhai Village, Jingzhu Town, and 91 kilometers from Fengjie. The mouth of the pit is 1,331 meters high, and the pit is 666.2 meters deep. The mouth and the bottom of the pit are 626 meters and 522 meters in diameter respectively. The pit is surrounded by steep walls. A small path on the northeastern wall leads to the bottom. There are two terraces on the wall: one is 300 meters deep and two to ten meters wide, another 400 meters deep. The slanting terrace is covered by grass, plants, and wild flowers. Springs flow down on the wall, joining an underground river, four kilometers long, at the bottom. Both the pit and ground crack belong to the same karst geological system. The underground river disappears in the Labyrinth Gorge. The Natural Pit at Xiaozhai is known as one of the cave wonders in the world.

The natural pit at Xiaozhai.

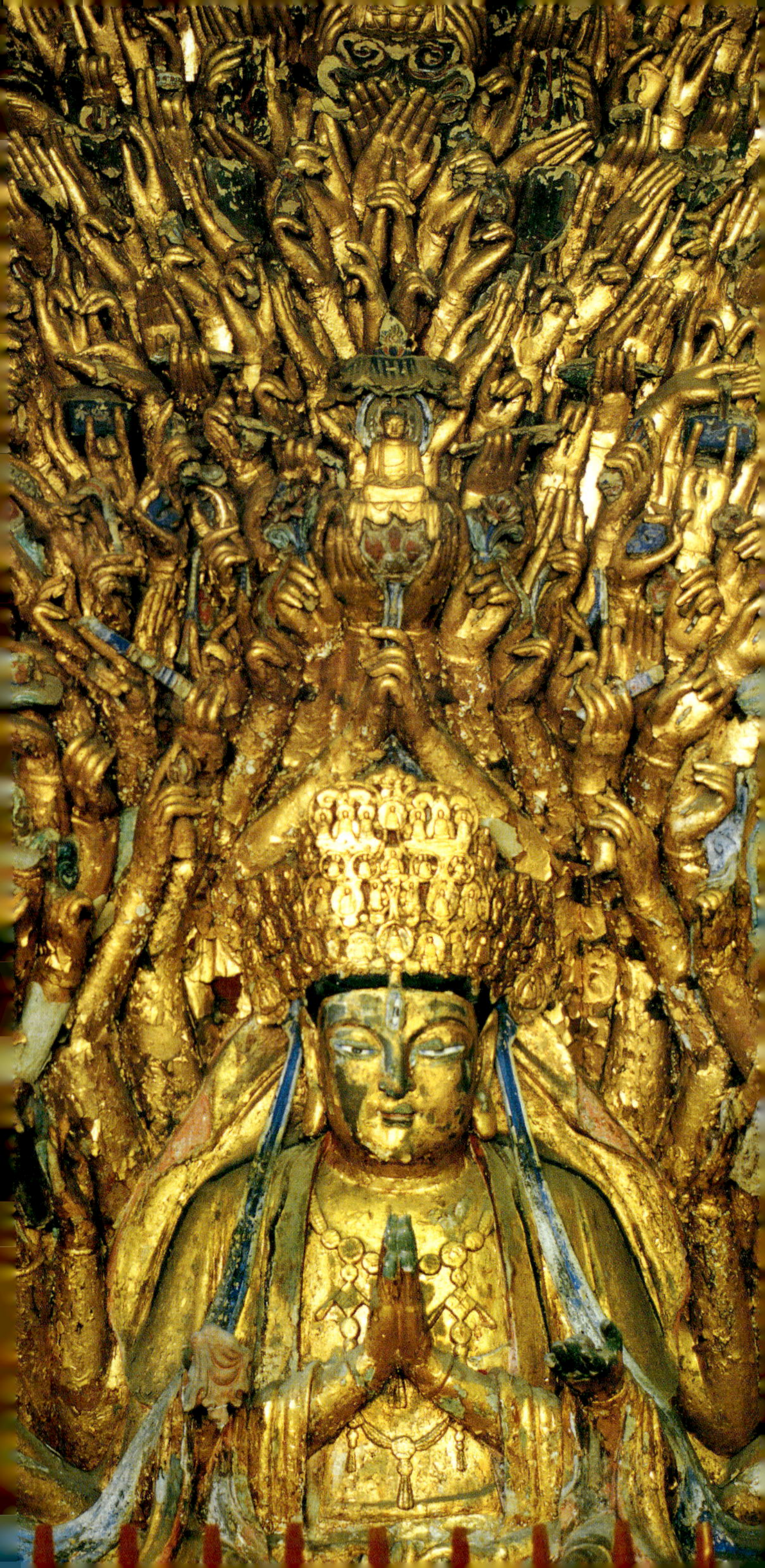

Dazu Stone Carvings Tourist Area

This Tourist Area includes Yongchuan City and the counties of Dazu, Tongnan, Tongliang and Bishan. It mainly features stone carvings of the Tang and Song Dynasties as well as natural landscapes and places of cultural interest. Some 87 kilometers from Chongqing proper, the Dazu Grottos showcase more than 100,000 stone carvings in 70 places, among which the most famous are cliff carvings on Mt. Baoding and Beishan. The art of stone carvings started in the late Tang Dynasty and reached its heyday in the Song Dynasty. The majority of the stone carvings are Buddhist statues, and the rest Confucian and Taoist statues. They are the best example of the art of stone carvings in the late period in China, and occupy an important position in religion, the arts, history, and culture, large in scale and rich in content, and represent the artistic level of Buddhist statues in China. Dazu Stone Carvings has been cited as a state Grade AAAA Scenic Area, and was put on the list of World Cultural Heritage in December 1999. The cliff carvings on Mt. Baoding and Beishan are among the first group of relics under major state protection; while those on Mt. Nanshan, Shizhuan, Qianfo, Shimen, and Miaogao, are relics under major municipal protection.

Cliff Carvings on Mt. Baoding

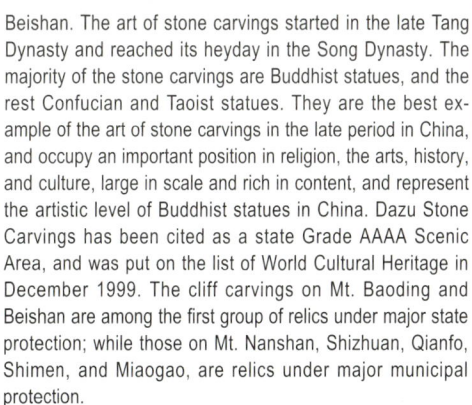

The cliff carvings on Mt. Baoding are found 15 kilometers northeast of Dazu County. In 1179, the sixth year of Emperor Chunxi's reign during the Southern Song Dynasty, eminent monk Zhao Zhifeng built a temple of grottoes, and the construction lasted for more than 70 years. Mt. Baoding is one of the sacred places for Buddhism in China.

The stone carvings are mainly found in Dafo (Giant Buddha) Bay. There are 13 places worth visiting, such as

Zhao Zhifeng (1159~1249)

A native of Changzhou, Dazu County today, Zhao Zhifeng is the founder of the stone carvings on Mt. Baoding. Zhao became a monk at the age of five and traveled around for three years when he was 16. He returned home in 1179, the sixth year of Emperor Chunxi's reign and participated in the construction of Shengshou Temple so as to preach. As requested by the rites place, he arranged, designed thousands of Buddhist statues in Dafo Bay in Mt. Baoding, the last large-scale grottoes in Chinese history.

Goddess of Mercy in No. 136 Grotto, Mt. Beishan.

Manjusri in No. 136 Grotto, Mt. Beishan.

Sakya Nirvana in No. 11 Grotto, Mt. Baoding.

Avalokitesvara of the Sun and Moon in No. 136 Grotto, Mt. Beishan.

Cliff carvings in Mt. Beishan.

the Lesser Buddha Bay, Dao Pagoda, the Hill of Dragon's Head, and Huangjiaopo in the east; the Tall Goddess of Mercy in the south; Mt. Guangda, Songlin Hill, and Fozu Rock in the west; and the Rock Gulf, the Dragon Pool, and Face-to-Face Buddha in the north. The most massive and intact stone carvings are in Dafo Bay.

The 500-meter-long Giant Buddha Bay is a mountain bay in the shape of a horse's hoof. On the 15- to 30-meter-tall cliffs are more than 10,000 stone statues, big and small. There are also seven stone tablets recording the construction of the Temple and Buddhist history, 17 scriptures of the Song Dynasty, and two stupas.

The stone carvings at the Giant Buddha Bay are unique and imaginative, superb in technique, and strong in local cultural flavor. There are 19 Buddhist statues on the cliffs in the east, north, and south, as well as poems, and Buddhist scriptures, elegant and rich. Major Buddhist statues include Protector of the Buddha Dharma or Buddhist Doctrine, Three Saint Buddha-Avatamasakas, the 1,000-Hand Avalokitesvara, the Hell, the Rites of Complete Enlightenment, and the Rites of Ox Herding.

Scientific techniques have been used for drainage, lighting, mechanics, and anti-weathering to protect the stone carvings.

Cliff Carvings on Mt. Beishan

Also known as Longgang, Mt. Beishan is located two kilometers north of Dazu County. In 892, the first year of Emperor Zhaozong's reign of the Tang Dynasty, a village named Yongchang was established at the foot of the mountain, to store grain and station troops when Buddhist statues were carved on the cliffs. The carving lasted for two dynasties, the Five Dynasties and Song, and nearly 10,000 Buddhist statues were carved. The majority of stone carvings on Mt. Beishan are Buddhist statues in 290 grottoes on the 300-meter-long, seven-meter-high cliff. There are also six steles, 55 inscriptions on the construction of the grottoes, eight Sutra-Pitakas, one relief of Manjusri, a Budhisattva of Mahayana Buddhism, receiving a patient, and 264 stone niches.

The exquisitely carved Buddhist statues are delicate and unique in style. The statue of Samantabhadra, Bodhisattva of Universal Benevolence, is reputed as Venus in the Orient. The statues of Goddess of Mercy Counting the Beads, and

Tourist Attractions

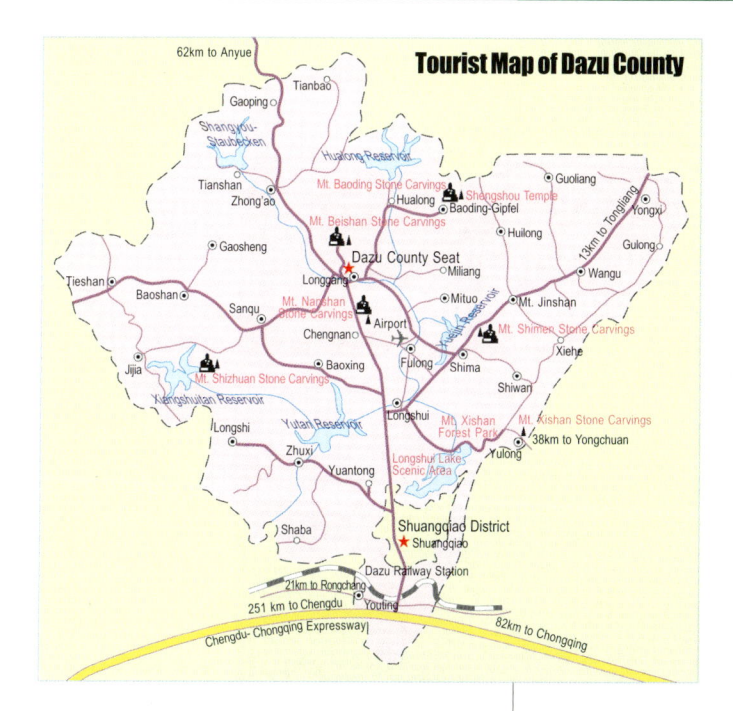

Tourist Map of Dazu County

the Goddess of Mercy of the Sun and the Moon represents the superb craftsmanship of stone carving in ancient China. The Zhuanlun Tripitaka Cave is known as the Stone Carved Palace; the Steles of Wei Junjing, Cai Jing, and Xiaojing are rarities in the world both as calligraphic treasures and valuable historical materials.

The Dafo Bay Grottos consists of two districts, the south and the north. Most of the statues in the southern district were carved in the late Tang period and Five Dynasties; while those in the northern district are works of the Song Dynasty. The Tang figurines are dignified and well rounded with graceful lines, while the Five-Dynasties figurines are cute and delicate in both appearance and dresses.

On the mountain slope facing the Dafo Bay stands a pagoda, known as White Pagoda, which was erected in the Southern Song Dynasty. An octagonal, brick structure, it has 13 stories outside and eight stories inside, totaling 33 meters high; and is a symbolic structure of Dazu County. There are 127 Buddhist statues, vivid and exquisite. Stairs inside lead to the top, where one can get a panoramic view of its surrounding areas.

Shengshou Temple

Located at the right back of the Dafo Bay, the Temple was first built by eminent monk Zhao Zhifeng in the Southern Song Dynasty, when it was known as Precipice of Five Buddhas. It was rebuilt during the Ming and Qing Dynasties.

The North Pagoda.

Shengshou Temple.

The Dragon Water Lake.

The temple on the mountain slope consists of the Hall of Heavenly Kings, the Hall of Jade Emperor, the Hall of Divine Inspiration, and Mahavira Hall. The Temple attracted quite a number of worshippers and pilgrims during the Ming and Qing Dynasties, and carved Buddhist statues are found on the walls, which are taken as the blueprints for those in the Dafo Bay.

Longshui Lake

Longshui, or Dragon Water, Lake lies at the northern foot of Mt. Beishan, 20 kilometers south of Dazu County. It was so named because of its location.

A man-made lake, it covers an area of 2,960 *mu*, 12.5 meters deep, three meters wide, and 525 meters long. The 108 natural islets are ideal home for water birds. The lake has been reputed as the West Lake in Dazu for its vast and crystal-clear water. Recreational facilities for water games, such as surfing and motorcycling have also been built.

The Western Hill on the lakeside covers an area of 23.92 million square meters. In the virgin forest there are rare and precious species of plants, such as dove tree and spinulose tree fern, which are under major state protection, and 60 species of animals and birds, such as rasses and egrets. There are tourist attractions, such as the Garden of Spinulose Tree Fern, the Bamboo Sea, and the Black Bamboo Grove Gully.

Black Dragon Lake

The Black Dragon Lake lies in the mist of mountains, 29 kilometers northwest of Bishan County. There are dozens of scenic spots, with a total area of 50 square kilometers, and 400 to 800 meters above sea level.

The Black Dragon Lake covers 230 *mu* in area with lush vegetation along the lakeside. The water in the lake is crystal clear. Traveling on the lake, one can enjoy the picturesque scenery along the lakeside. Standing on a small islet, one can admire the beautiful scenery of the lake. People can also visit the local farmers and enjoy the authentic local food there.

Tourist Attractions

Giant Buddha Temple, Tongnan

Formerly named Nanchan or Dingming, the Giant Buddha Temple is situated at the foot of Mt. Dingming, 1.5 kilometers northwest of Tongnan County. A wooden structured ancient building complex, it consists of four structures, including the Giant Buddha Pavilion, the Hall of Goddess of Mercy, the Hall of Jade Emperor, and Jianting Pavilion.

The Giant Buddha Pavilion was built by water at the foot of the mountain. A giant statue of Sakyamuni, 18.43 meters high, is enshrined in the Pavilion. The statue was made in 874, the last year of Emperor Xiantong's reign during the Tang Dynasty.

On the cliffs in the east and west of the Giant Buddha are 83 inscriptions, poems, and stone carvings by famous personages and men of letters of past dynasties, 20 golden-plated inscriptions, five hydrological inscriptions, 104 niches, and 700 Buddhist statues. On the red cliff not far from the Temple there is a Chinese character, "佛", 50 square meters in area, the largest of its kind in China. It was carved during the reign of Emperor Tongzhi of the Qing Dynasty.

There are 18 scenic spots around the Temple, such as the 1,000-Buddha Rock, the Washing-the-Face Rock, and carved Taoist statues.

The Giant Buddha Temple in Tongnan.

Mt. Malong bathing in the setting sun.

Cliff Carvings on Mt. Malong

Also known as the Tongnan Reclining Buddha, the cliff carvings are found on the northern side of Mt. Malong, 40 kilometers south of Tongnan County.

The carved Buddha is 36 meters in length, with his eyes closed, his head to the east, and facing north.

On the cliffs 80 meters from the Reclining Buddha there are 198 niches for Buddhist statues and three niches for Taoist statues. Numbering 700 in total, the statues were evenly carved with graceful figures. The 500 arhats are especially vivid and unique in style.

Ancient Town of Shuangjiang

The ancient town of Shuangjiang is located 10 kilometers northwest of Tongnan County, with the Fujiang River and the Grand Canal passing by. All structures are of the Ming and Qing styles, which can be seen from the gates, pillars, walls, eaves, and courtyards. Flowers and plants are luxuriant all year round. Shuangjiang is a typical township with an appeal of the Ba culture.

The ancient town of Shuang-jiang, Tongnan, has well-preserved building complex of the Qing Dynasty.

Mt. Bayue

Standing at the juncture of the counties of Dazu and Tongliang, Yongchuan City, and Shuangqiao District, the mountain consists of 35 peaks. The scenic area covers 50 square kilometers, and its average elevation is 778 meters.

A stone-laid path on the southern side leads to the top of the mountain, known as Incense Burner Peak. Standing on the Incense Burner, one can see the rolling hills like a dragon in the distance. There used to be nine temples in the mountain, and only four of them still stand firm. By the Bayue Temple there is a 30-meter-tall ancient cypress, approximately 1,000 years old. It is known as Guest Greeting Cypress.

Tiandeng Rock on Mt. Bayue.

Mt. Bayue features a typical karst land formation. The clear spring and excellent vegetation depict a magnificent view of natural beauty.

Dragon Hot Spring Holiday Resort

The Dragon Hot Spring Holiday Resort touches Tongliang County, 78 kilometers from Chongqing.

The hot springs have a daily output of 5,000 cubic meters; and they contain high hydrogen sulphide and elements, such as fluorine, strontium, and boron, which can cure skin diseases. The annual, constant temperature is 42°C, or above. The Holiday Resort has an area of 450 *mu*, with 500 guestrooms, 80 hot spring pools, a standard swimming pool, and a conference hall with 600 seats. It is large enough to accommodate 20,000 visitors.

Tourist Attractions

Chongqing Wildlife Park

The Chongqing Wildlife Park is located in Shuangzhu Town, eight kilometers south of Yongchuan. It covers an area of 30 square kilometers, and is a state-class ecogarden and tourist area specializing in wild animals.

The complicated geological environment offers favorable conditions for wild animals.

Among its 30,000 animals of 430 species, 10,000 of 260 species have been classified as Grade I and II under international protection and Grade I and II under state protection. The Park consists of five districts, the Area for Visitors Traveling by Cars, the Area for Pedestrians, the Square, the Rear Service Center, and the Parking Lot. More than 20 exhibition areas are opened, where visitors can see tigers, bears, leopards, crocodiles, parrots, birds, and amphibians.

Gemsboks and giraffes.

Mountain of Tea & Sea of Bamboo

The Mountain of Tea & Sea of Bamboo is located on the mountain range of Qishan. It is 33 kilometers long, and occupies an area of 116 square kilometers, six kilometers north of Yongchuan City and 64 kilometers from downtown Chongqing.

Mt. Qishan is covered by vast tea trees, bamboo groves, and ancient trees. It is a municipal-level forest park, and 97 percent of its slopes are covered by trees.

The Mountain of Tea has fresh air and 20,000 *mu* of tea trees. On the mountain there is a Tea Art Mountain Villa, which consists of the Exhibition Hall of China's Tea Culture, the Sightseeing Teahouse, the Food Center, the Pottery Art Hall, and the Hotel. Visitors can learn more about China's tea culture through picking up, making, sipping, and eating tea.

A bamboo grove in Mt. Qishan.

The Sea of Bamboo covers some 50,000 *mu* in area, where more than 10 species of bamboo are planted. It consists of six districts, and is dotted with the Golden Basin Lake and Tongziwan Reservoir. The crystal-clear springs add a miraculous power to the bamboo groves.

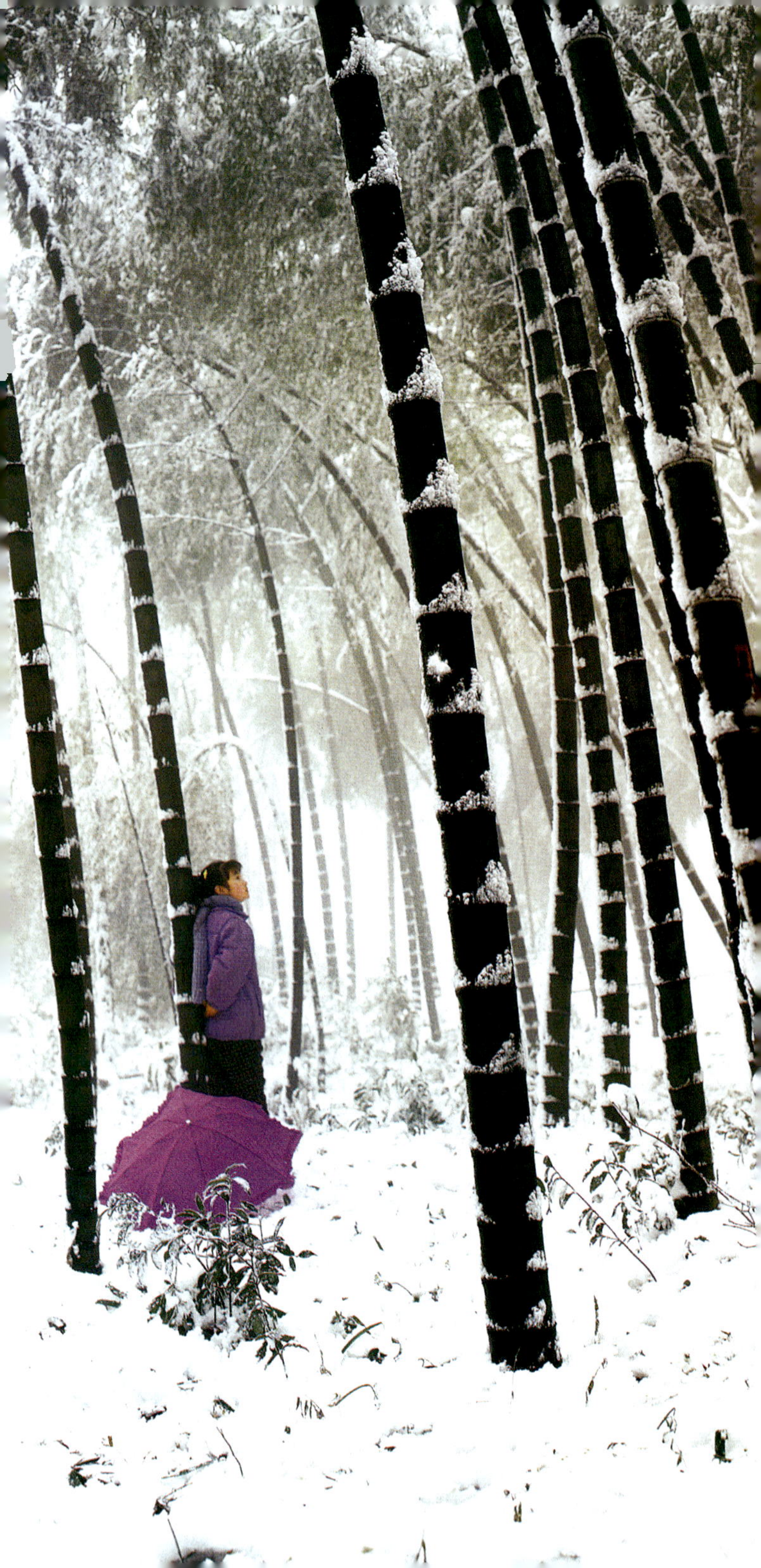

Tourist Attractions

Mt. Jinyun Tourist Area

This Tourist Area consists of Hechuan City and Beibei District. It is the best place to enjoy the natural landscape with state-level scenic spots, such as Mt. Jinyun and the Ancient Battlefield in Fishing City, as well as places of interest, such as the Lesser Three Gorges on the Jialing River, the Golden Knife Gorge, and the ancient township of Laitan.

Mt. Jinyun

Also known as Mt. Bashan, Mt. Jinyun stands along the Wentang Gorge of the Jialing River in the Beibei District. It was a result of the Yanshan Movement some 70 million years ago. Today, it is a state-level natural scenic spot, along with other tourist attractions, including the Lesser Three Gorges on the Jialing River and the Fishing City in Hechuan. It consists of nine peaks, among which Yujian is the tallest, 1,050 meters above sea level, and Shizi, or Lion, is the most magnificent and dangerous.

Mt. Jinyun is a national nature reserve with extremely mild weather and abundant rainfalls. More than 1,700 species of sub-tropical plants are found in its 13 million square meters of forest, such as ginkgoes, Ormosias, and a moth tree with two wings growing out of its fruits. There is also metasequoia, an extremely rare living fossil of tree, as old as 160 million years.

Mt. Jinyun is believed to be holy for Buddhists, with a history of more than 1,500 years. Jinyun Temple was first built in the Southern Dynasty, and it had been praised and conferred with titles by emperors of all past dynasties. The Jinyun Academy in the temple was established long time ago. The Temple collects 24 Sanskrit scriptures read by Emperor Taizong of the Song Dynasty. Outside the Temple is a wall, four by four meters, with relief of unicorn, lions, and white elephants, a relic left behind of the six dynasties. A stone archway of the Ming Dynasty stands by the wall.

Northern Hot Spring Park

It is located in the Beibei District, with the Jialing River in the north and Mt. Jinyun in the south. Formerly known as the Hot Spring Temple, which was first built in the Southern Dynasty and rebuilt in 1432, the seventh year of Emperor Xuande's reign of the Ming Dynasty, it was established in 1927, when known as Jialing River Hot Spring Park. It was later renamed as Chongqing Northern Hot Spring Park, when tourist facilities, such as hot spring swimming pools, bathrooms, and dining rooms were added.

The Park consists of four halls, including Guansheng, Jieyin, Giant Buddha, and the Goddess of Mercy. Guansheng, or Three Saints, serves as the gate of the temple. Right behind

Chongqing to Mt. Jinyun Tourist Area of the Fishing City and Ancient Battlefield

Buses No. 502 and 508 at Niujiatuo, No. 503 at Chaoyangmen, No. 504 at Yangjiaping (get off at Beibei, and shift Bus No. 518 to Beiwenquan, or a long-distance bus to Hechuan) in Chongqing are available to all tourist attractions in this Tourist Area.

Jinyun Temple.

The Lion Peak on Mt. Jinyun.

Hot Spring Temple

Formerly a part of the Jinyun Temple, it used to be magnificent with numerous carved stone statues. Unfortunately, it was destroyed during the reigns of Emperors Wudi of the Northern Zhou Dynasty and Wuzong of the Tang Dynasty. It was reconstructed during the reign of Emperor Zhenyuan of the Tang Dynasty, when cliff carvings were made at the back of the Temple. In 1007, the fourth year of Emperor Jingde's reign during the Northern Song Dynasty, when it was entitled Chongsheng.

The Temple reached its heyday during the Ming and Qing Dynasties, when reconstructions were undertaken. More attractions, such as Fish Pond and the Crescent Moon Pond, were built by using the resource of hot spring and the terrain.

the Jieyin Hall is a square pool formed by springs. On the balustrades of the bridge over the pool there are patterns of unicorns, plantains, flowers, and birds carved in the Ming Dynasty. The Hall of Giant Buddha enshrines a Buddhist statue of the Ming Dynasty. The Hall of Goddess of Mercy features stone pillars and iron tiles.

To the east of the four halls there are gardens, such as Guxiang, or Ancient Fragrance, and Shike, or Stone Carvings. Guxiang Garden is the site of the Hot Spring Temple, with ancient trees and tombs of three generations of monks during the Song, Ming, and Qing Dynasties. In Shike Garden, there are stone steles of the Song, Ming, and Qing Dynasties, among which the Coiling Dragon Tower of the Ming Dynasty is a treasure.

There are 10 springs in the Park, with a daily output of 5,675 tons. The temperature is between 35°C and 37°C and the hot springs are effective for the diseases of the skin, joints, and digestive systems.

Recreational items, such as bungee, skating, and parachuting on water, have been developed over the last few years.

Tomb of General Zhang Zizhong

The tomb is located on Mt. Meihua in the Beibei District. On May 16, 1940, General Zhang Zizhong devoted his life to a war against Japanese invaders in Yicheng, Hubei Province; and his body was brought back to Beibei and buried at the foot of Yutai Mountain. The tomb, 2.64 meters in height and 21 meters in girth, covers an area of 3,267 square meters. The stone was inscribed by General Feng Yuxiang. In 1982, the State Council posthumously admitted Zhang as a revolutionary martyr. A few years later, the municipal government of Chongqing established a cemetery and a memorial hall. The cemetery is a state-level cemetery as well as a center for patriotic education.

Zhang Zizhong (1890~1940)

Styled himself Jinchen, Zhang Zizhong was born in Linqing County, Shandong Province. He joined the army in 1914 and was promoted as commander of an army group and ranked General Second Class. He devoted his life to the country in May 1940 during the Anti-Japanese War.

Former Residence of Lao She

The Former Residence of Lao She is located at 61 Tiansheng New Village, Beibei District. It is a villa in Chinese and Western styles. There are eight rooms on the first floor, with an area of 120 square meters. It was formerly the residence of Lin Yutang. In 1943, Lao She moved in, and wrote some one million Chinese characters for his operas, including *Zhang Zizhong* and the *Peaches and Plums in the Spring Breeze*, and novels, including *Four Generations Under*

One Roof and *Cremation*. It used to be a gathering place for literary giants. Today, a Memorial Hall to Lao She has been established in front of the Residence, showcasing 160 works and documents by Lao She, 160 photos, and stationeries and articles used by him. The Residence is now a relic under municipal protection.

Ancient Town of Pianyan

Located in the Beibei District, the township of Pianyan was established in the late Ming Dynasty, with traditional structures along both sides of the streets laid with stone slabs. The ancient town of Pianyan is charming with wooden houses, old-fashioned theaters, and trees over 300 years old.

A lake known as Shengtian is 3,000 kilometers from the town. It is an ideal resort to escape the summer heat.

The ancient town of Pianyan.

Golden Knife Gorge

The Golden Knife Gorge.

Lying at the southwestern foot of Mt. Huaying, the Golden Knife is 6.2 kilometers, and consists of two parts, the upper and the lower. The upper part consists of odd rocks and waterfalls, and the lower stalagmites and stone pillars in various gestures. A five-kilometer-long ancient plank road stretches in the valley.

A stream runs through the valley, sometimes like a galloping horse. It becomes a pond in the depth of the gorge. There are seven ponds and five shoals, and the water in the ponds are blue, purple, or black, and cold.

Ruins of Dinosaur Fossils. Beibei

Chongqing used to be a home to many dinosaurs, a fact that has been proven by the fossils discovered in 30 ruins in 12 districts, counties, and cities, among which Beibei is the most famous. From 1939, when the first bone fossils of dinosaurs were found at Jingangbei, through 1982, when three dinosaur fossils were discovered in Jianshe Village, 13 ruins of four species of dinosaurs have been unearthed.

Fishing City

Covering an area of 2.5 square kilometers, the Fishing City is located on Mt. Diaoyu, or Fishing, on the southern bank of the Jialing River in Heyang Town, Hechuan City. The Fishing City features overhanging peaks and imposing, solid city gates and walls; and it is surrounded by three rivers, Jialing, Fujiang, and Qujiang on three sides. It used to be a place of military importance. The well-preserved ancient battlefield has been listed as a relic under state protection as well as a national tourist attraction.

The Fishing Terrace.

In 1242, the second year of Emperor Chunyou's reign during the Southern Song Dynasty, Yu Jie, then mayor of Chongqing, gave instructions to build the Fishing City. In

The Site of Ancient Battlefield in the Fishing City

The Fishing (Diaoyu) City is surrounded by water on three sides; and the ancient battlefield is still well preserved. There are ruins, such as city gates, city walls, imperial palace, government offices, army camps, and harbor, as well as tourist attractions, such as the Fishing Terrace, Huguo Temple, Xuanfo Temple, the 1,000-Buddha Grottoes, the Emperor's Cave, the Heavenly Spring Cave, and the Flying Eave Cave. Legend has it that immortals used to live here. There are a great number of poems, relief, and stone tablets of the Yuan, Ming, and Qing Dynasties. In 1982, the Fishing City was made a state-level scenic spot.

1258, the troops of Mongolian Khan Mengge invaded Sichuan and stationed outside the Fishing City in February 1259. The invaders could hardly conquer the Fishing City thanks to the unremitting resistance of the army led by Wang Jian and Zhang Yu. In July, Mengge was badly injured by the gun fire and died in the Hot Spring Temple. The defensive war lasted for 36 years through 200 fierce battles, writing a brilliant page in history concerning wars in China and the world.

Huguo Temple in the Fishing City was built in the Song Dynasty, and is now an exhibition hall, displaying relics of the City. There are statues of historical personages, including Wang Jian and Zhang Yu, and merit steles of heroes. An ancient osmanthus tree, 21 meters tall and 1.9 meters across, stands in the Garden of Shigui in the Temple. A stone archway, 10 meters in height, is found in front of the gate. It was erected during the Ming Dynasty, with four Chinese characters, "独钓中原". In front of the Temple is a Fishing Terrace, on which lies a stone statue of Buddha carved in the Song Dynasty. To the west of the Reclining Buddha is the 1,000-Buddha Rock, 20 square meters in size, where 2,772 Buddhist statues, each measuring 8 centimeters high, are found. They were carved in 1272 of the Southern Song Dynasty.

Wentang Gorge of the Lesser Three Gorges.

The Lesser Three Gorges in the setting sun.

Lesser Three Gorges, Jialing River

Stretching for 27 kilometers long, the Lesser starts from Juliang Shoal and ends at Badou Woods. It consists of three gorges, including Libi, Wentang, and Guanyin.

The Libi Gorge is located in Yanjing Town, Hechuan, and is three kilometers long. The river in this section is deep and rapid.

The Wentang Gorge, also known as Wenquan, or Hot Spring, is located in Mt. Jinyun, and is 2.7 kilometers long. There used to be hot spring pools known as Wentang, at the narrows. Hence its name. The rapid water rushes into the gorge and forms whirlpools. The narrowest point between the sheer cliffs on both sides is only 200 meters. Springs pulls down halfway the cliffs.

The Guanyin Gorge is also known as Wenbi, 3.7 kilometers in length. It is the most dangerous section among the three gorges. A huge rock stands at the narrows, by which there is an ancient temple, named the Pavilion of Guanyin, or Goddess of Mercy, on the sheer cliff. Hence the name of the gorge. The river zigzags through the gorge, and a railway and a cable highway bridge span over the river.

Ancient Town of Laitan

The ancient town of Laitan is 40 kilometers northeast of Hechuan, and was built in the Song Dynasty. To protect itself from foreign invasions, a stone city wall was built on the cliffs during the reign of Emperor Jiaqing of the Qing Dynasty, forming a world of 0.25 square kilometers surrounded by a wall, 1,380 meters long and two to three meters tall. Among the four city gates, three are well preserved. During the reign of Emperor Tongzhi of the Qing Dynasty, an enceinte was built outside the city gate to reinforce the defense of the city. The enceinte, semicircled, seven meters tall, 2.5 meters wide, and 40 meters long, is the only well-preserved ancient defense in Sichuan and Chongqing.

The ancient town of Laitan.

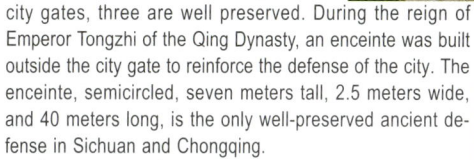

There are 400 Qing-style residences in Laitan and two streets laid with stone slabs. One street runs between the city gate in the middle and the small city gate, another leads to Erfo (Two-Buddha) Temple and ends at the small city gate in the east. Places of historic interest include stone archways erected during the Ming Dynasty, Twin-Pagoda built during the Qing Dynasty, the Opera Theater at Wenchanggong, and the Peace Pond against fire.

Erfo Temple

Erfo, or Two-Buddha, Temple, is located by a canal in Laitan, 40 kilometers northeast of Hechuan. It is a municipal-level scenic spot as well as one of the Top Ten Scenic Spots in Chongqing. The cliff carvings in the Temple are exquisite and superb, a rarity of carved Buddhist statues in China. As early as 1956, it was announced among the relics under major protection in Sichuan.

Erfo Temple.

First built in 881 of the Tang Dynasty, it covers an area of 10,000 square meters, and consists of two parts, the upper and the lower. The Upper Hall stands on top of Jiufeng Peak, and the Lower Hall is a two-storied tower. The statues on the cliffs in the Temple were carved during the Song Dynasty. There are 1,600 Buddhist statues in 42 grottoes on the cliffs in the west, north, and south. The largest statue is Sakyamuni, 12.5 meters tall, with his head 6.32 meters across, hand 2.13 meters long, and feet 6.25 meters from one another. It is known as the Giant Buddha. There are groups of Buddhist statues around the Giant Buddha, including Kasyapa Buddha, Dasabhumi Bodhisattva, six founders of the Zen Sect, and numerous arhats and monks.

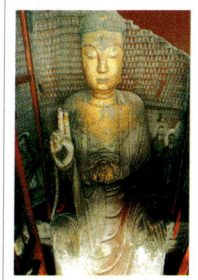

The Giant Buddha in Laitan.

飛泉

Tourist Attractions

Suburban Hot Spring and Lake Holiday Resort

The Suburban Hot Spring and Lake Holiday Resort consists of the districts of Banan, Beibei, and Yubei, and the counties of Changshou and Bishan. There are tourist attractions, Tongjing Hot Spring, Northern Hot Spring, Southern Hot Spring, Eastern Hot Spring, Changshou (Longevity) Lake, and Bayu Folklore & Culture Village.

The waterfall in the Southern Hot Spring.

Southern Hot Spring Scenic Area

The Southern Hot Spring Scenic Area is situated among the hills near the Huaxi River south to the Yangtze River in the Banan District, 18 kilometers from the downtown area. The scenic spots include the Southern Hot Spring Park and the ruins of Jianwen and auxiliary capital.

The park is well known for its hot springs. The sulfur hot spring descends from Mt. Jianyu, and the water temperature is around 40°C, with an output of 120 tons an hour. The bath pools were first built during 1862 and 1874, the reign of Emperor Tongzhi of the Qing Dynasty, and some swimming pools were added after the Liberation.

Apart from hot springs, there are also five famous springs in the scenic area, such as the Jade Spring, the Bright and Rainy Spring, the Dragon Spring, the Flying Spring, and the Spring of the Roaring Tiger.

During the Anti-Japanese War, senior KMT officials, such as Lin Sen, He Yingqin, and H. H. Kung, built their villas here. People can also see the former KMT political university and the president's office of Chiang Kai-shek.

The Huaxi River adds a decent touch to the scenic area.

Eastern Hot Spring Scenic Area

The Eastern Hot Spring Scenic Area in the Banan District, 68 kilometers from the city proper, is abundant with natural wonders—hills, waters, forests, springs, waterfalls, gorges, and caves—and places of cultural and historic interest. There are 24 scenic spots, including the Hot Cave, the ancient plank road, and the Wubu River. There is a hot spring on the lower reaches at the narrows of the Guanjin Pass, which is believed to be holy by the local people. It is a unique custom that men and women take baths in this hot spring together without feeling shy or uneasy no matter what season it is. In the ancient White Sand Temple there is a tree known as Eighteen Halves, over 100 years old, in an odd situation: half alive and dead, half dry and wet, half covered and exposed, half straight and inclined, half old and young, and half joyful and sad. There are also other ancient temples built after the Ming Dynasty, in addition to places of interest, such as the New Village of the Anti-Japanese War, Fudan Middle School, and the Tomb of Yang Cangbai.

South Lake

The South Lake is located in the Banan District, 30 kilometers from the downtown area. Also known as Nanpeng

Southern Hot Spring Scenic Area
Take Bus No. 302 at Wuyi Road.

The Holiday Resort.

Jianwen Peak
Jianwen Peak is said to be a place where Jianwen sought asylum because Zhu Di, the fourth son of Emperor Zhu Yuanzhang, seized the crown and turned out to be the emperor, which should have been passed on him. Jianwen died here; and the locals built a temple in his honor.

Ground Sledges
With a full length of 1,888 meters, ground sledge system is for fun seekers and exercisers.

The cableway in Jianwen Peak.

Eastern Hot Spring

There are 48 springs, and the temperature of the water is 42°C. The water contain high hydrogen sulphide and elements, which can cure skin diseases. At the foot of Mt. Mu'er there is a cave, 100 meters long, with hot springs of 40°C contain high. It is reputed as a natural sauna because of the slow ventilation.

To go to the Eastern Hot Spring, take Bus No. 386 at Daomenkou, Yuzhong District.

South Lake

Many buses can take you to this place.

Qiaoping Ancient Village

The Qiaoping Ancient Village, with an area of 27 square meters, was built amidst the cliffs. Since the Tang Dynasty, it has served as a defense against foreign invaders. More defensive works, such as city walls, were built in the late Song Dynasty. The village was completed, with a total of 48 village gates during the reign of Emperor Guangxu of the Qing Dynasty, half of which still stand firm after many wars.

Mt. Qiaoping

Take a bus at Nanping.

Reservoir, it is a man-made lake, with an area of over 1.3 million square meters, the largest of its kind around Chongqing. Today, it has become a lake for irrigation, water supply, aquatic cultivation, and tourism.

Hemmed in by mountains with lush vegetation and fresh air, the South Lake is equipped with up-to-date tourist facilities, including 50 boats for travelers to enjoy the landscape on the lake side.

South Lake Fishing Village

The Village is located in the middle of the Carpe Island with accesses to other peninsulas in the lake area. The unique layout, the special scenery, the state-of-the-art facilities, and the local flavor make the Village a final destination for holiday makers.

Qiaokouba

It is located at the juncture of the townships of Baijie and Yipin, Banan District, 34 kilometers from Chongqing. People can enjoy the snaking streams and rolling hills alongside by boat.

The rich hot spring resources, with a water temperature of 41°C, make Qiaokouba an ideal choice for hot spring bath, recuperation, and recreation.

Mt. Qiaoping

Mt. Qiaoping covers 25 square kilometers in area, at an average elevation of 650 meters. It is situated in Lujiao Town, Banan District. Ma'an Peak, the highest peak, stands 750 meters above sea level. Looking up the slope, one can see the mountain towering loftily in the middle of the basin; When one steps onto the mountain top and takes a bird's-eye view of the surrounding areas, he can feel the mounds and hillocks almost the same height while packing with each other, with an amazing view of vast forest, crisscrossing lakes, springs, terraced fields, and tea plantation.

Qiaoping has long been well known for its ancient villages, temples and tombs. During the Song Dynasty, the mountain became a sacred place for Buddhism with 48 temples, among which Tiancheng, Chaodeng, and Baiyun were built in the Northern Song Dynasty. There are also many places of

Tourist Attractions

historic interest.

There are quite a number of ancient tombs on the mountain, of which the majority are of the Ming and Qing Dynasties. The most famous and best-preserved tombs are the Tomb of Manzi on the General's Range and that of Liu Chunjun, minister of Rites of the Ming Dynasty.

Mt. Shengdeng Forest Park

Located in the south of the Banan District, 70 kilometers from the Yuzhong District, the municipal-level Forest Park possesses a great species of plants.

Mt. Shengdeng is the highest peak in southern Chongqing. Its main peak stands 1,064 meters above sea level, with sheer cliffs and unique geographical structure, which can be seen from the varied peaks, cliffs, and rocks.

Jiangjia Limestone Cave Scenic Area

Located in the Banan District, 70 kilometers from Chongqing proper, the limestone caves have been reputed as the Long Corridor of the Arts Underground. So far, two caves, the Mist and Dew and the Dragon Pool, are opened. There are more than 100 attractions in seven scenic areas in the 800-meter-long Mist and Dew Cave. The Dragon Pool Cave, 2,500 meters long, consists of nine scenic spots.

Outside the Dragon Pool Cave there are ruins of the Diyuan Society of Poems, Wantian Palace, and the Palace of King Yu the Great.

Tongjing Gorge Scenic Area

Located by the riverside of Yulin, Yubei District, this scenic area has 10 square kilometers in area. It features unique scenery among other tourist attractions in Chongqing, and was made one of the city's first Top Ten Scenic Areas in 1998.

The Tongjing Gorge consists of three gorges, including Wentang, Tongjing, and Laoying. The lush bamboo groves on the sheer cliffs of the gorges are home to numerous wild

Dragon Pool Cave

Outside the Cave there are three waterfalls available for bathing all year round because the water is cool in summer and warm in winter. Seven villages built during the Ming and Qing Dynasties stand on the mountain ridge, the best place to watch the sunrise and the sea of clouds.

Jiangjia Limestone Cave Scenic Area

Take Bus No. 386 at Daomenkou and get off at Jiangjia.

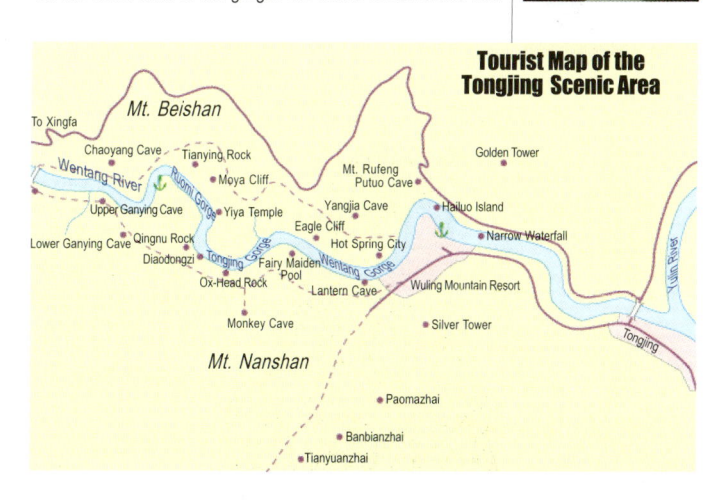

Tongjing Gorge.

Young sailors at Tongjing.

Tongjing Gorge Scenic Area

Buses at the Northern Bus Station are available to this scenic area.

Tongjing Hot Spring City

There are 26 natural hot springs in Tongjing. The water temperature averages from 35 to 53 °C, and the highest 62°C. It contains rich mineral elements, such as strontium, fluorine, lithium, hydrogen, radon, calcium sulfate, and edible silicic acid, which have curative effect and are good for health. There are also service facilities, such as outdoor swimming pools for both adults and children, indoor swimming pools for lovers and couples, a parking lot, a ballroom, a sitting hall, a buffet for cold drinks, and a health center.

An old-fashioned bed.

Local Folklore & Cultural Village

Take Bus No. 608.

A stone archway erected during the Qing Dynasty.

monkeys and eagles. During the reign of Emperor Qianlong of the Qing Dynasty, the place was cited as one of the Top Twelve Scenic Spots in Sichuan Province. There are also heaps of limestone caves, among which Xiaganying, Yangjia, and Monkey are the most famous.

Modern tourist and recreational facilities have been added, such as the 56-meter-high terrace for bungee jump, the 800-meter-long runs for carting cars, and facilities for parachute challengers. Accommodation and food are also available in the scenic area.

Local Folklore & Cultural Village

The Local Folklores & Cultural Village in Lianglu Town, Yubei District, covers an area of 50,000 square meters. It features simple, old-fashioned buildings with painted walls, grey tiles, and bamboo fences around the thatched cottages.

The Museum in the Village showcases more than 1,000 handicrafts, garments, and articles for daily use, among which 250 pieces are eye-catching. They include home-made niches, inscribed horizontal boards, and wooden-carved beds, tables, chairs, and desks, all made during the late Qing Dynasty. The museum also collects 200 pieces of wooden carvings, root carvings, and wall hangings. The four courtyards of the Museum, varied in styles and layouts, display rites and customs of the ancient Ba people concerning birthdays, wedding ceremonies, funerals, and festivals, as well as production procedures of farming and manual crafts-manship. An ancient temple to the Goddess of Mercy exhibits various religious activities of the ancient Ba people. An archway erected in 1904, the 30th year of Emperor

Tourist Attractions

Guangxu's reign of the Qing Dynasty can also be seen in the village.

There are other places of interest and tourist facilities, such as a cable bridge, a square, a lake, farm houses, the teahouse, and the folklore street.

Zhangguan Limestone Cave

Located in Zhangguan Town, Yubei District, 69 kilometers west of the Yuzhong District, the Limestone Cave enjoys convenient transportation. The scenic area covers an area of nine square kilometers, and consists of a natural limestone and an underground river. The natural cave measures 4.6 kilometers long and has an underground river running all year round and various gestured stalactites.

Outside the cave are the natural sightseeing and places of historic interest, such as the gully, mountain villages, and ancient battlefields. There is also a 720-meter-long course, 85 meters above the ground, for parachuting.

A wedding ceremony of the Tujias.

Longevity Lake

Longevity Lake, a man-made lake built in the 1950s to cut off the Longxi River, is located in eastern Changshou (Longevity) County, 28 kilometers from the county seat. The average depth of the lake is 15 meters, and the deepest measures 50 meters. The Lake is now the largest lake scenic area in Chongqing.

The Lake has vast expanse of water, and is surrounded by rolling hills on all sides. The tallest peak is 770 meters above sea level, the best place to watch the sunrise and the sea of clouds. There are more than 200 islets in the lake, which is home to many species of fish. Don't be surprised if a big fish jumps onto your boat when traveling. During the late spring and early autumn, the lake attracts more than 10,000 birds, such as swans, egrets, white cranes, wild ducks, and gulls.

There are orchids in the lake area all year round. The large space on the lakeside draw many sports fans for water games and parachuting.

Longevity Lake in the morning.

Parachuting over the lake.

Longevity Lake

Take a bus at Niujiaotuo or Hongqihegou Bus Station in Chongqing and get off at Changshou. Shift a bus to Shizitan and stop at the lake area. It's usually an hour's drive.

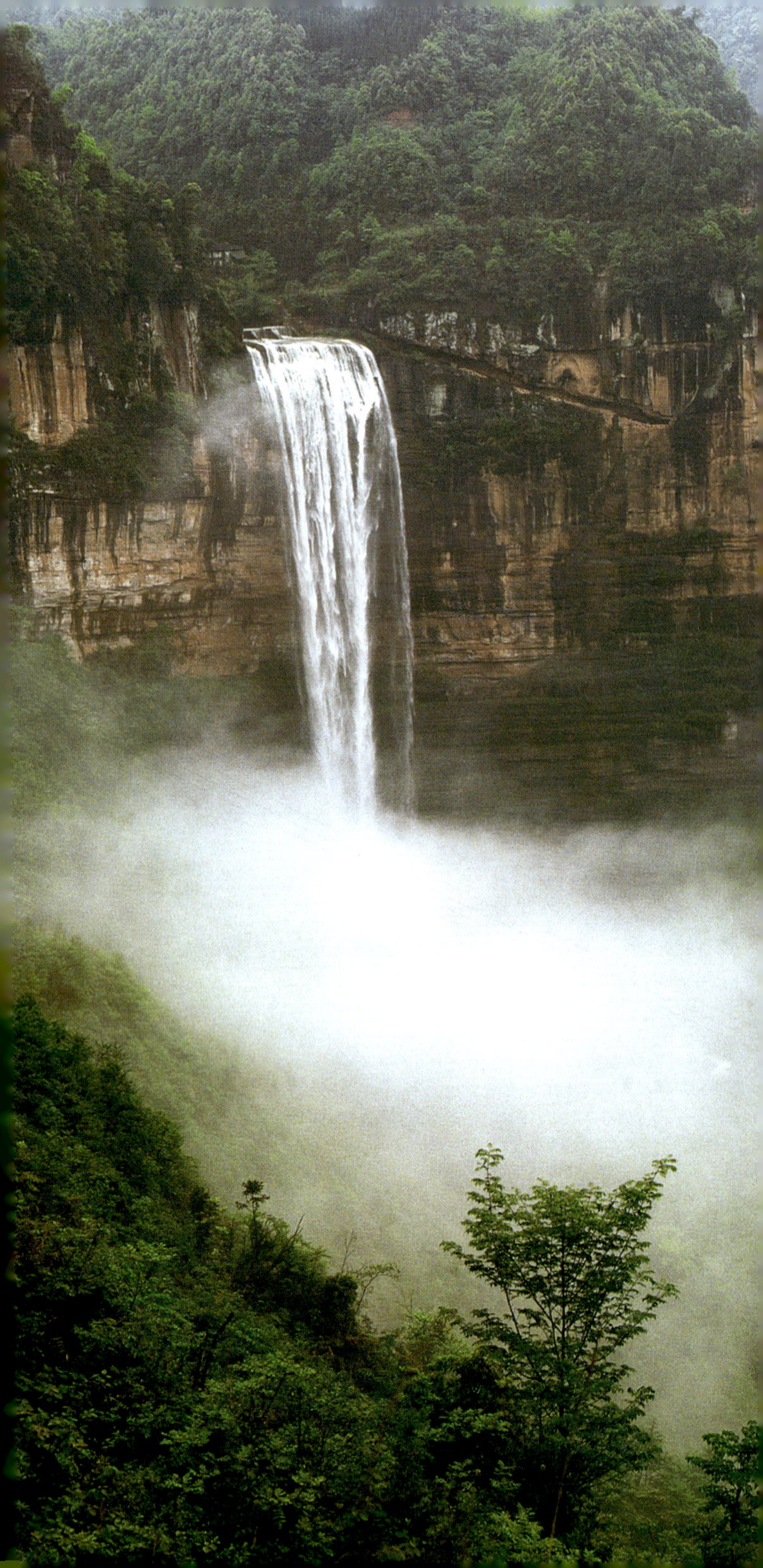

Tourist Attractions

Ecological Tourist Areas of Mt. Simian, Mt. Jinfo, and Wansheng Stone Forest

This scenic area consists of national scenic spots of Mt. Simian and Jinfo and the Wansheng Stone Forest in the cities of Jiangjin and Nanchuan, Qijiang County, and Wansheng District, where visitors can enjoy the natural beauty, learn about the local customs, and escape from the summer heat.

Mt. Simian Scenic Area

Mt. Simian, or Four-Sided Mountain, is located in Jiangjin City, 140 kilometers from Chongqing. Geographically, it is defined as a mountain upside down. The terrains of the mountain in the north are lower than those in the south. Wugong, or Centipede, Peak is the highest among others, 1,709.4 meters above sea level. The lowest peak is 560 meters above sea level. Covering area of 240 square kilometers, the climate belongs to subtropical monsoon, with an annual mean temperature of 13.7 °C and an average rainfall of 1,522.3 millimeters.

The Scenic Area mainly features virgin forests, along with 40 streams and brooks, eight alpine lakes, and 100 waterfalls. Lakes such as Dragon Pool, Vast Sea, and Capital of Forest, are inlaid on the endless forests, shining brightly like pearls. The waterfall known as Watching the Hometown drops 152 meters down, and is the highest waterfall in China. The waterfall near Shuikou Temple, 94 meters tall, is suspended below a natural cave. Featuring a typical karst land formation, the mountain is home to various species of plants and animals. The primitive broad-leaved forest is better preserved in comparison with those on the same latitude. More than 1,500 species of plants and 19 species of plants on the verge of danger find home here, the most precious of which is spinulose tree fern, as old as 350 million years. Among its 207 species of wild animals, 40 are rare, such as macaques, clouded leopards, red-chested pheasants, zibets, and rasses. There are 120 scenic spots in the mountain scenic areas, such as the Toudao River, the Xiangshui Shoal, and Shuikou Temple.

Mt. Heishi

Mt. Heishi is 2.5 kilometers from Baisha Town, Jiangjin, and the scenic area covers 22 square kilometers in area. There are 540 black rocks on the mountain top, the largest of which measures hundreds of square meters, and the smallest nearly 10 square meters, in size.

On the mountain stands the Jukui Academy, built in 1880, the sixth year of Emperor Guangxu's reign during the Qing Dynasty. It preserves more than 50,000 volumes of ancient Chi-

Mt. Simian Scenic Area

Buses at the Chongqing and Yangjiaping Bus Stations shuttle between Chongqing and the scenic areas of Jiangjin and Mt. Simian. There are also trains and boats that can take you to Jiangjin, where you can change a bus to Simianshan Town.

The waterfall on the Terrace of Watching the Hometown in Mt. Simian, Jiangjin.

The waterfall at Shuikou Temple.

Map of Mt. Simian

Honghai Lake.

Spinulose tree fern.

Azaleas in Mt. Jinfo.

nese books, most of which are 100 years old. On the summit is the Henian Hall in the European style of ancient Roman theaters, the largest of its kind in eastern Sichuan. During the Anti-Japanese War, many celebrities, including Chen Duxiu, Feng Yuxiang, Wen Youzhang, and Ouyang Jian lectured or delivered speeches here.

Mt. Gujian Forest Park

Located 10 kilometers from Qijiang County, Mt. Gujian is part of the Dalou Mountains in Guizhou Province. The Forest Park stretches 1.8 kilometers from north to south and 1.4 kilometers from east to west, at an elevation of 1,000 meters.

Rivers wind their way dozens of kilometers through the magnificent mountain, a home to countless white cranes. Halfway the mountain slope there is an ancient village with dense trees. The time-honored Jingyin Temple on the mountain top still attracts many pilgrims and visitors. At the back of the Temple there is a stone, arch bridge, known as Yangqiao. It was erected during the reign of Emperor Jiajing of the Ming Dynasty.

Mt. Changtian Forest

Thirty-six kilometers from the county seat, Mt. Changtian stretches for 70 kilometers. The central area is a virgin forest, 500 square meters in area with many species of plants, and untouched for over 100 years. The mountain is unique in shape, thus featuring various landscapes.

Dingshan Lake

Located in Dingshan Town, Qijiang County, the lake is three kilometers long and one kilometer wide. It is enchanting with secluded hills, tranquil water, dangerous cliffs, and grotesque waterfalls.

Mt. Jinfo Scenic Area

Located 15 kilometers south of Nanchuan City, Mt. Jinfo, or Golden Buddha, is an eastern offshoot of Mt. Dalou. It consists of three mountains, including Jinfo, Baizhi, and Jingba, and its tallest peak is 2,251 meters above sea level.

Mt. Jinfo has virgin forests with luxuriant trees and deep valleys. It is known as a Kingdom of Natural Plants, including many rare species and plants of 1,000 years old.

In the Scenic Area there are over 100 peaks and more than 10 odd caves. Major tourist attractions are the Golden Buddha Cave, the Lesser Stone Forest, the South Heavenly Gate, and the Satin Screen Peak. There used to be 200 temples in the mountain, but only a couple of them have been left, such as the Golden Buddha, the Phoenix, the Iron Tile, and the Lotus.

The Old Buddha Cave is found in the central area of the mountain top. The entrance is narrow, and the 48-zigzagging path leads to a huge, spacious hall, 46,000 square meters in area, which is large enough to hold 10,000 people. Standing at the entrance, one can see the Fairy Maiden Cave on the cliff as well as the northern slope of the mountain.

The Lesser Stone Forest, three kilometers from the Old Buddha Cave, gathers odd-shaped peaks, stone pillars, and stone screens, accompanied by ancient plants. Walking along the path, one can enjoy the fantastic works of art by nature.

In the Longyan River at the northern foot of the mountain there are three hot springs of different temperature, known as Triple Springs. Swimming pools of hot springs have been built by the highway of Sanquan (Triple-Spring) Town. In 1939, Chiang Kai-shek and his wife visited the place and had a bridge, later known as Mei-ling, erected over the river. A small mountain path leads to historic sites during the Anti-Japanese War.

The Reclining Dragon Pool Gorge is situated on the northern

Animal Museum in Mt. Jinfo

The Museum is located in Xipo, Mt. Jinfo, with an area of 2,000 square meters. It consists of three halls, including Animals, Plants, and Rare Species of Plants.

Mt. Jinfo has enjoyed a fame of the Kingdom of Plants. There are 5,880 precious and rare species of 333 families of plants, 250 species of which are very ancient, 136 species special, 82 species endangered, and 52 species rare; in addition to four species under state Class I protection, 18 species under state Class II protection, and 30 species under state Class III protection. Five species of plants, including spruce, ginkgo, big-leaved tea, square bamboo, and azalea, are the most famous in the mountain. The vast virgin forest is home to 523 species in 150 families of animals, 37 species of which are under state protection. The animals under state Class I protection include leopard, south China tiger, white-combed crane, red-chested pheasant, golden monkey, and Sika deer. The Museum displays over 6,000 samples of plants and animals collected from Mt. Jinfo.

The Reclining Dragon Pool.

Mt. Jinfo Scenic Area

Take a bus at Chongqing and Yangjiaping Bus Stations, get off at Nanchuan, and shift a bus to the scenic area. Also available are special tourist buses.

The King Azalea, 3.2 meters across.

mountain slope. An overpass between sheer cliffs leads to the untouched virgin forest. A brook winds its way down the valley.

The Green Pond and Secluded Ravine are located in Xipo. The Ravine zigzags for 10 kilometers. This scenic area features rapid streams, twisting rattans, and lush forests. Steep cliffs stand one next to another.

Mt. Nanzhu Forest Park

The Forest Park is a natural summer resort, 15 kilometers from downtown Nanchuan, and has bamboo groves and rolling hills. There are tourist attractions, such as the Zoo, the Hexagonal Pavilion, the Spring of the Goddess of Mercy, and the Temple of Fragrant Clouds.

Wansheng Stone Forest

Wansheng Stone Forest
The special tourist train departs at 8:00am from the Railway Station. Buses are also available at the Nanping Bus Station.

Located in Nantian Town, Wansheng District, the Stone Forest is 20 kilometers from the Wansheng District. Standing 730 to 820 meters above sea level, it was form-ed during the Ordovician Period, the most ancient stone forest in China, and is of high value for the geological study of the Sichuan Basin.

The Stone Forest features typical karst land formation, with many stone pillars and mushroom-shaped peaks. Some of the peaks resemble birds and flowers, and geologists have reputed the place as a "naturally-made paradise of animals".

In the northeast of the scenic area there is a stele forest, known as the Stele Forest of World Peace, where stand tens of memorial stone tablets.

Mt. Heishan Primitive Eco-Tourist Area

Mt. Heishan Scenic Area
Take a bus at Wansheng.

Located 20 kilometers from the Wansheng District, this tourist area features high mountains, dense forest, and crisscrossing streams and brooks. Remaining untouched, it has balanced ecological system of subtropical and temperate zones of the same latitude, 97 percent of which are covered by forest. Specialists appraised it as a "bio-genetic base in Chongqing and Sichuan" because it is the largest area with balanced primitive, eco system. The mountain valley stretches for 13 kilometers, with a 6-kilometer-long cable way leading to the summit, a 6-kilometer-long plank road, and a floating bridge.

Tourist Attractions

Map of the Wansheng District Scenic Area

- Jinqiao
- Nanchuan
- Conglin
- Qijiang
- White Dragon Lake Scenic Area
- District Government Office
- Hot Spring Scenic Area
- Wansheng
- Nantong
- Heishan Ravine Ecological Tourist Area
- Jingxing
- Nantian
- Qingnian
- Tongzi
- Shilin-Landschaftsgebiet
- Guanba
- Jiuguojing Scenic Area
- Tonggu Beach
- Podu
- Changtangkou
- Podu River
- Tonggutan Rafting Scenic Area

Distance: Wansheng - Tourist Attractions
20km to Stone Forest
23km to Mt. Heishan
38km to Jiuguojing
58km to Tonggutan
10km to Hot Spring
20km to White Dragon Lake

Legend
- District Government Office
- Town, village
- Boundary
- Scenic area
- Major highway
- Highway section

Rafting along the Tonggu Shoal Valley

Tonggu, or Bronze Drum, Shoal is located in Guanba Town, 40 kilometers west of the Wansheng District. Rafting can start from Changtangkou in Podu Town, Guizhou Province, last for 11.2 kilometers, and end at Tonggu Shoal in the Wansheng District. The water in this section flows swiftly, the shoals high, the valley secluded, and the water clear. Traveling in rubber dinghies with the help of experienced sailors, the rafting will be exciting and romantic.

Rafting along the Tonggu Gorge

Take a bus at Wansheng and get off at Guanba. Change a minibus and stop at the starting point of the adventurous rafting.

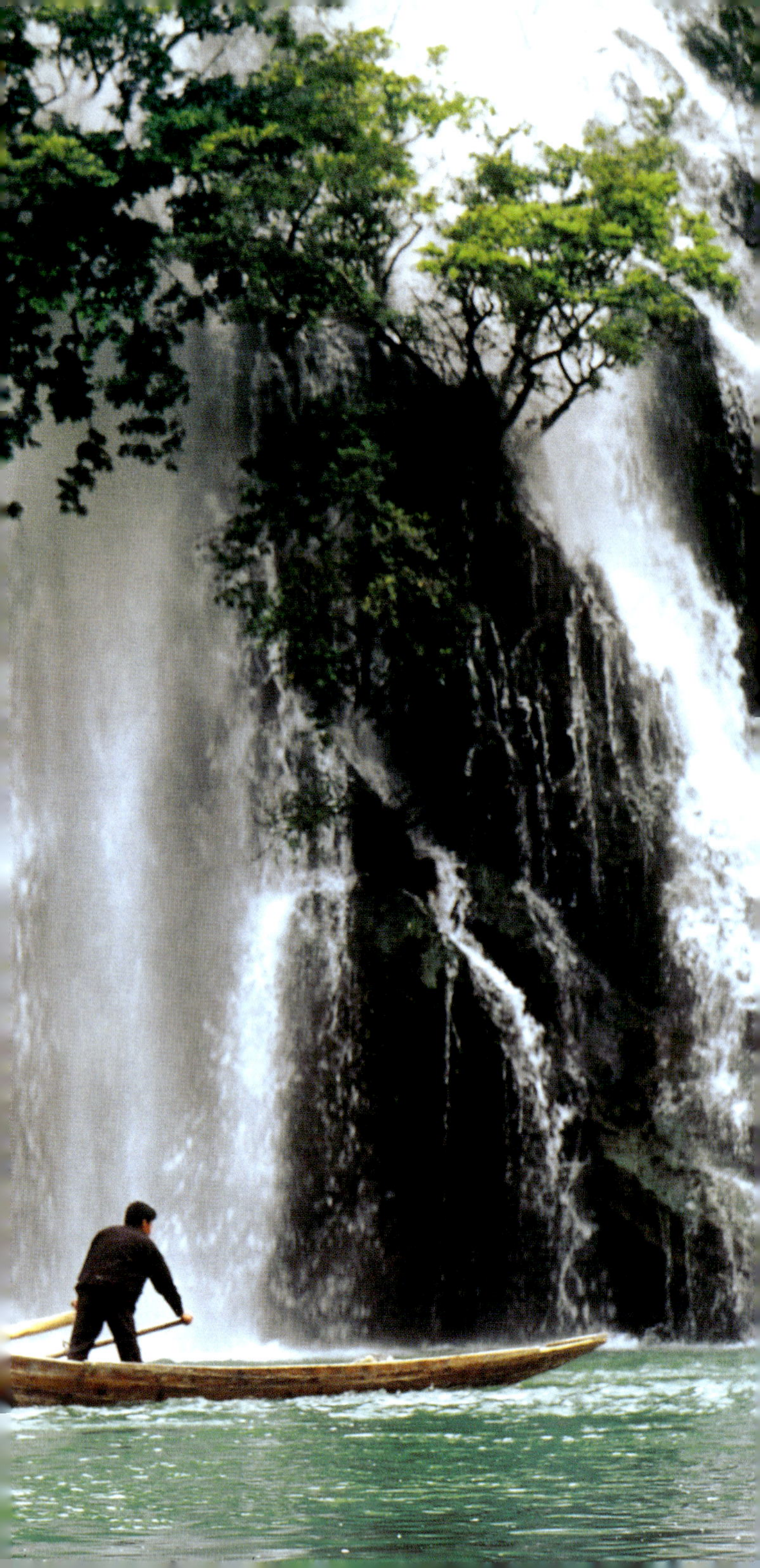

Tourist Area of Mt. Fairy Maiden & Lotus Cave

This tourist area mainly features the wonderful scenery in the Lotus Cave, Rafting along Huangbai Ferry, Mt. Fairy Maiden, and the Wujiang Gorge.

Lotus Cave

The Lotus, a state Grade AAAA tourist area, is located four kilometers from Jiangkou Town, Wulong County. It is so huge that it has been regarded as a "world geological wonder." The many on-the-spot surveys jointly made by geologists from China, Britain, US, and Ireland prove that the cave is the most densely located cave group in China. Daxiao, the deepest cave, stretches for 430 meters, and is 110 meters high, with the longest underground waterfall in China. There are underground rivers, fossils of ancient living creatures, and underground lakes—a rarity in the world. In addition, there are gypsum crystals, the largest of its kind in the world. There are much more in the cave, waiting to be uncovered, hence leaving enough space for adventurers.

A world of stalactite in the Lotus Cave.

The Lotus Cave, 2,700 meters long, was discovered in May 1993. After the explorations by specialists from relevant organizations in China and Australia the cave was appraised as a World Wonder, a Grade A Cave Scenic Spot, a Palace of the Arts Underground, and a Museum of Cave Science. The stalactites inside the cave covers almost all 30 kinds of deposits in the world, among which the most amazing scene are the stone "waterfalls" and "curtain", 15 meters wide and 21 meters high. The palm-like stalagmites are as clean and bright as jade, and the twisting stones and stone flowers shimmer like stars. It is rare to see so many, beautiful shapes of stones, so fine in quality and so widely distributed. The red coral and the canine-tooth calcite crystal in the pool are even more precious. There are some 30 scenic spots in the cave, such as the Huge Screen with Flying Waterfalls, the Canine-Tooth Calcite Crystal, the Marine Dragon Palace, and the Pearls in the Field of Stones, to name only a few.

Skiing on Mt. Fairy Maiden.

Parachuting Across the Furong River

A double-way, the adventure starts from Jiangkou Town, Wulong County. A single trip is 669 meters or 779 meters, 300 meters above the river. Special safe belts are made for challengers, who can enjoy the picturesque view of the gorges on the river as well as the panorama of the power station.

Mt. Fairy Maiden

Mt. Fairy Maiden (Xiannu) Forest Park is located in Shuanghe Town, 33 kilometers from Wulong County. The mountain is part of the Wuling Mountain Range. Looking from a distance, it resembles a fairy maiden wrapped with fog.

Mt. Fairy Maiden, an alpine pastureland, has a forest of 300,000 mu and a grassland of 100,000 mu. It is reputed as Switzerland in the Orient for its natural landscape.

Above the mountains, 1,900 meters above sea level, are alpine grasslands and small ridges; and the highest peak is 2,033 meters high. Forests cover more than 300,000 *mu*, and the pasturelands 100,000 *mu*. The Forest Park is attractive for its four wonders: the sea of forest,

The Qinglong Bridge in Wulong.

The People's Square in Wulong.

Wulong County

Wulong County has long been known as a Place of Vital Importance on Land and Water because of its geographical location. It used to be a poverty-stricken area. However, China's implementation of the reform and opening-up policies has brought dramatic change to the county on its way to prosperity.

Transportation between Chongqing and the Lotus Cave
One way to go to Wulong is to take a bus at Chaotianmen Bus Station, and another is to to go by boat.

The Moon Gate

The Moon Gate is found at the foot of the Fairy Maiden Rock along the eastern bank of the Wujiang River in Qingshui Town, Wulong County. Looking through the gate, one seems to see a full moon hung over the sky.

Map of Communication & Location of Mt. Fairy Maiden, Lotus Cave, and Furong River

grotesque peaks, pasturelands, and snow forest. The landscape here is enchanting all year round.

There are tourist attractions, such as Houjiaba Pastureland, the Sea of Forest, the Pastureland, the Holiday Resort, the Tent Village, Wild-flavor Hot-pot Town, and the Hunters' Village. Over the last few years, more recreational facilities have been added for car racing, horse racing, archery, skiing, bonfire, BBQ, mountaineering, paintball shooting, and parachuting.

Tiansheng Three Bridges

A state-level AAAA scenic area, the Three Bridges, including Tianlong, Qinglong, and Heilong, are located in Wulong County, 20 kilometers east of the lower reaches of the Wujiang River. The average height of the three bridges is 300 meters, and they are 100 meters wide each. Some 1.2 kilometers from the bridges spans a naturally-formed stone arch bridge over the deep valley, which can be hardly found elsewhere in the world.

Rafting from Huangbai Ferry

It is an exciting adventure to raft from Huangbai Ferry on the Changtu River, three kilometers from Wulong County. The section between Huangnicao and Huangyu Gorge is about eight kilometers, along the banks of which are farm houses and paths laid with rocks and bamboo. A rubber dinghy is big enough to hold two or three challengers, who can sail by themselves through gorges and shoals.

Rafting along the Furong River.

Tourist Attractions

Folklore Tourist Area of Qianjiang & Wujiang

This tourist area covers five Tujia and Miao autonomous counties, including Qianjiang, Youyang, Xiushui, Pengshui, and Shizhu. Major tourist attractions are the Lesser South Sea, Nanyaojie, and Land of Peach Blossom. It is the place to enjoy natural landscape, learn about ethnic customs, and pay respect to martyrs. It is also an important gateway to the scenic area of Zhangjiajie. Qianjiang county is 400 kilometers from Chongqing and 300 kilometers from the Fuling District.

Lesser South Sea

Located in the rolling mountains, 32 kilometers north of Qianjiang, the Lesser South Sea features wonderful natural landscapes of mountains, rivers, islands, and gorges.

The Lesser South Sea is a well-preserved site of earthquakes in ancient China. In May 1856, the sixth year of Emperor Xianfeng's reign during the Qing Dynasty, this place was attacked by a severe earthquake, which broken rocks and cliffs as well as a dam built with stones. Today, the place is a national reserve for earthquake sites as well as a center for the dissemination of earthquake prevention and disaster relief.

The Lesser South Sea is hemmed in by beautiful peaks and lakes dotted by islets of lush bamboo groves, where people can see cottages and bamboo houses and hear crowing and barking.

A wedding ceremony of the Tujias.

The Folklore of the Tujias

Between the third and the 15th day of the first lunar month, the Tujia people in the Qianjiang area hold grand sacrificial ceremonies to pray for good harvest and celebrations to welcome the New Year, during which time they enjoy their hand-waving dance overnight. The dance is originated from a dance in ancient Chongqing and Sichuan, depicting the rites, ceremonies, and work, and it has a strong rhythm and graceful steps.

The Tujia people are clever and deft, and good at brocade weaving. They show their love for nature, express their feelings for life, and record mother's love and their passion for lives, and tell legendary stories, through weaving. The weavings cover a wide range of life and the craftsmanship is superb.

The Lesser South Sea is a well-preserved ruins of earthquake in ancient China.

The ruins of the earthquake.

The Ruins of the Old Stone Age, Laowuji

The ruins is located at Laowuji Cave in Fengjiaba, Qianjiang County. During the excavation between December 17 and 28, 1985, fossils of some 100 species of animals were brought to light, including six families and 20 genera of mammal animals and five species of extinct animals, such as gibbons, oriental stegodons, and Chinese rhinoceros, and 800 stone articles dating back to the mid and late Old Stone Age. The discovery of the ruins is of great significance for the study of the prehistory in the Qianjiang River regions as well as the geological history of the Quaternary Period.

Ancient Town of Longtan

The street laid with stone slabs in Longtan.

Located at the junction of the Wujiang and Apeng Rivers, Longtan is 30 kilometers southeast of Youyang County; and it is one of the ancient townships with well-preserved structures built during the Ming and Qing Dynasties in Chongqing. There are places of historic interest, including the Palace of King Yu the Great, the Longevity Hall, the Catholic church, the 3-kilometer-long street laid with stone slabs, 50 timber and bamboo houses supported by wooden stakes over ground of the Tujias, 150 fire walls, 200 one-story compound houses, and the Former Residence of Zhao Shiyan, built in the 28th year during Emperor Guanxu's reign.

Dayou Cave & Land of Peach Blossom

Dayou Cave in Youyang, a state Grade AAAA tourist area.

Located about one kilometer from the county of Youyang, with an elevation of 670 meters, the cave is a big, natural limestone cave, 30 meters high and wide, and 180 meters long. In the cave, one can see streams and stalactites. Four Chinese characters, "太古藏书" inscribed by Luo Shengwu, governor of Youyang during the Qing Dynasty,

Tourist Attractions

can still be seen on the wall. Leaving the cave, one can see a small basin, 40,000 square meters in area surrounded by hills on all sides. A brook runs through the basin. Along the brook sides are peaches and rice fields. The spring at the bottom of the basin runs all year round, echoing with the springs falling down from the caves on the cliffs. The brook at the bottom of the basin passes through Dayou Cave, finally joins the Youyang River.

From Chongqing to Qianjiang

Take a long-distance bus from Chongqing, or take a boat from Fuling to Pengshui, and shift a bus.

Ancient Town of Gongtan

It is located at the western end of Youyang County, north of the junction of the Apeng and Wujiang Rivers, and faces Guizhou Province on the other side of the Wujiang River. Established some 1,700 years ago, the ancient township features timber and bamboo houses supported by wooden stakes over ground, streets laid with stone slabs, and ancient bridges.

Construction of timber and bamboo houses supported by wooden stakes over ground started from the Southern Song Dynasty, a special view of Gongtan. The houses have two or three stories.

The ancient town of Gongtan has a 2,000-meter-long street, entirely laid with stone slabs and polished by history. There are cliff carvings, square wells of 700 years old, and many bridges, big and small.

Wujiang River, a Natural Beauty

The Wujiang River descends from the Guizhou Plateau and runs northeastward through the mountain ranges of Dalou and Wuling. Stretching for 1,050 kilometers, it passes through 46 counties and cities in Sichuan and Guizhou Provinces, and empties itself into the Yangtze River at Fuling.

The charm of the Wujiang River lies in its cave, rivers, and gorges. The cave is known as Lotus; the rivers are referred to Furong, or Lotus, and Daxi, or Big Stream; the gorges are numbered seven, including Sanmen, Biantan,

Boats bathing in the setting sun.

Yanjing, Guantan, Zhongzui, Menshuan, and Luojiatuo. There are also other tourist attractions, such as the Tomb of the King of Ba, the Lesser Three Gorges of the Yajiang River, the ancient town of Baima, the ancient cave of the Goddess of Mercy, the Heroine Rock, and Guantan Shoal.

Traveling by boat along the river, one feels as if he were walking in a picture. The section that presents the best scenery of the river is between Pengshui and Youyang, 120 kilometers in length. There are 70 scenic spots in this section.

Carved Grave Stone at Dachewan

Located at Dachewan, Tongxi Town in Youyang County, the tomb was built in 1876, the second year of Emperor Guangxu's reign during the Qing Dynasty. An empty tomb, in fact, it is five meters long and four meters wide, and was built with rectangular stone slabs. In front of the tomb stands a stone inscribed with Chinese characters and relief. The stone carvings consist of nine layers on the upper, middle, and lower, 50 pictures in total to tell 40 stories from classics and legends. Moreover, there are also patterns of pavilions, terraces, trees and flowers, birds and fish, Chinese unicorns, and lions.

Site of the Third Red Army's Headquarters, Nanyaojie

Located 105 kilometers from Yujiatongzi, Nanyaojie Town in southern Youyang County, the site is a relic under provincial-level protection. It touches five counties in Chongqing and Guizhou. In 1934, under the leadership of He Long, the Third Red Army set up a special zone in eastern Guizhou, with Nanyaojie as the headquarters. In October the same year, the Sixth Red Army led by Xiao Ke, Wang Zhen, and Ren Bishi joined forces with the Second Red Army here.

The headquarters at Yujiatongzi, the former residence of Yu Lancheng, a scholar of the late Qing Dynasty, consists of 12 rooms, and is a wood-and-stone structure supported by wooden stakes above the ground, with an area of 450 square meters. During their stay here, the Red Army built a 2.8-meter-high, 278-

The Wujiang River.

Young ladies of the Tujias.

The tranquil, ancient, yet beautiful township of Hong'an, Xiushan County.

meter-long wall with rectangular stone slabs and bricks. In the courtyard there are two pear-leaved crabapple trees planted by He Long. In front of Yujiatongzi stands a memorial pavilion in memory of the joining forces of the Second and Sixth Red Armies, which was inscribed by Liao Hansheng. On the left is the cemetery of the Red Army men.

Site of the Ancient Tunnel Warfare, Qingxi

It is located in Wangle Village of Qingxi Town, 14 kilometers west of Xiushan City.

In ancient times, the Miao people in Xiushan used tunnels to fight against foreign invasions. In 1976, the local people of Xiushan found a zigzagging tunnel running from east to west, which is one kilometers long, 1.5 meters high, and 0.5 meters wide. There is a blindage every ten meters, with one mound on the wall for lights. The bottom is flat and the top is supported in the shape of an arch, allowing one person passing. Traces of oil and gas can still be seen on the wall. Iron weapons and tools to dig the tunnel were also found in the tunnel.

Huangshui Dafengpu Scenic Area.

Huangshui National Forest Park

This Forest Park is located northeast of the Tujia Autonomous County in Shizhu, with an average elevation of 1,550 meters. The highest peak is 1,934 meters above sea level. Because of the big difference of elevation, climate changes distinctively. Summer is cool and refreshing, making it an

Weaving a life of colors.

Folklore of the Miaos

The Miao people in Qianjiang County are talented singers and dancers, young and old, male and female. Songs are the most common way to express their feelings: they greet each other singing, tell stories with songs, and express love through music and lyrics.

Autumn Fair is a traditional festival of the Miao people, which falls on the Beginning of Autumn, usually on the 7th or 8th day of August, during which time people dress up and get together, singing and dancing, playing on the swing, competing the skills of climbing ladders of knives, showing dragon lanterns, and participating in singing contests. The Autumn Fair is a good opportunity for young people to their Mr. or Ms. Rights. There are also other festivals on the third day of the third lunar month, the sixth day of the sixth lunar month, the seventh day of the seventh lunar month, the Guomiao Festival, and the Sheep & Horse Festival. The Miao people are well known for their traditional arts and crafts, such as embroidery, wax dieing, and handicrafts.

ideal summer resort.

Not only the Forest Park has virgin forest but it also has precipitous peaks and beautiful rivers. Dafengbao Virgin Forest is the center of the Forest Park, with plants, flowers, and birds. It is the best preserved virgin forest in the Three Gorges area.

Bizika Green Palace is located in the Huangshui National Forest Park. It is a municipal Grade AA tourist area in Chongqing.

Huangshui Lake, 2.5 kilometers west of Huangshui Town, is a man-made lake built in the 1980s. It consists of four parts, hemmed in by green, rolling mountains.

Mausoleum of Qin Liangyu

Located seven kilometers east of Shizhu County, the mausoleum covers an area of 200,000 square meters. It was built in 1648, the fifth year of Emperor Shunzhi's reign during the Qing Dynasty. The Longhe River passes through and Mt. Huilong backs up. It consists of two tombs. It is said that there used to be 48 tombs, too many for people to distinguish which is real. There is a stone with inscriptions on merits of Qin Liangyu. There are 20 tombs of Qin's brothers, his descendants, and generals under her command. By the river there is a cave known as Immortal, where suspended coffins are placed.

Wanshou Village

The village of Wanshou, or Longevity, is 20 kilometers east of Shizhu County. At an elevation of 1,490 meters, it has grotesque, steep peaks. In the north and south of the village stand two stone pillars, one known as Man, another Woman. Qin Liangyu used to lead his men to fight for the village, leaving behind ruins of three village gates, which can be seen today. On top of the mountain there is a well,

A house supported by wooden staked above the ground.

Qin Liangyu (1574~1648)

Qin Liangyu is a famous woman general in the late Ming Dynasty. During her life time, Qin led her men to fight many battles, accounting for 45 years. She was awarded by the royal court many times for her triumphs, and her traces could be found in almost all parts of the country.

Singing along.

providing drinking water for tens of households. At the back of the village gate there is a cave, known as Immortal, which enshrines a couple of Buddhist statues. On the wall are three Chinese characters, "万寿山" inscribed by Qin Liangyu.

Green Tower

Located on top of a sheer cliff along the eastern bank of the Wujiang River, not far from Pengshui County, the Green Tower was built by Huang Tingjian, a noted poet, in 1094, the first year of Emperor Shaosheng's reign during the Northern Song Dynasty.

Based on a 10-square-meter huge rock in the shade of an old Banyan tree, the tower used to have four flying eaves, engraved doors, and low balustrades. Over the gate is a horizontal board with Chinese characters, "绿荫轩山谷书". On the wall of the base there are poems and inscriptions by men of letters of past dynasties. At the foot of the Tower there is a cave, resembling a reclining Buddha. Standing in front of the Tower, one can get a panoramic view of the surrounding hills and the Wujiang River.

Mt. Fenghuang

Towering three kilometers south of Xiushan County, Mt. Fenghuang, or Phoenix, is famous for natural landscapes. There are scenic spots, such as the Peach Blossom Cave, the Lotus Cave, Lingguan Hall, an ancient temple built in the Yuan Dynasty, the Tower of the Goddess of Mercy, and the Grand-View Pavilion. Around the Phoenix there are also places of historic interest, including Junfu Cave, a site of the Nine Streams & Eighteen Caves of the Yuan Dynasty in the east, the Water Lily in the Meijiang River in the south, the Fengming (Crowing Phoenix) Academy built in 1818, the 23rd year of Emperor Jiaqing's reign during the Qing Dynasty, in the west, and the Forest of Stalagmites in the north.

Stone Carved Chinese Character "寿"

It is said that the officials of Pengshui County contributed a stone-carved, red Chinese character "寿" (longevity) to the royal court as a present to celebrate Emperor Qianlong's 80th birthday. The emperor was pleased and wrote the same character as a reward. In fact, the character carved on the cliff along the bank of the Wujiang River, 157 by 123 centimeters, was inscribed by Zhong Lian, governor of Pengshui County, forceful and gorgeous. Many people have come to imitate the calligraphy, an example of which can be seen on the cliff of Erwang Temple in the city of Dujiangyan.

A house of the Miao people.

A local opera of the Tujias.

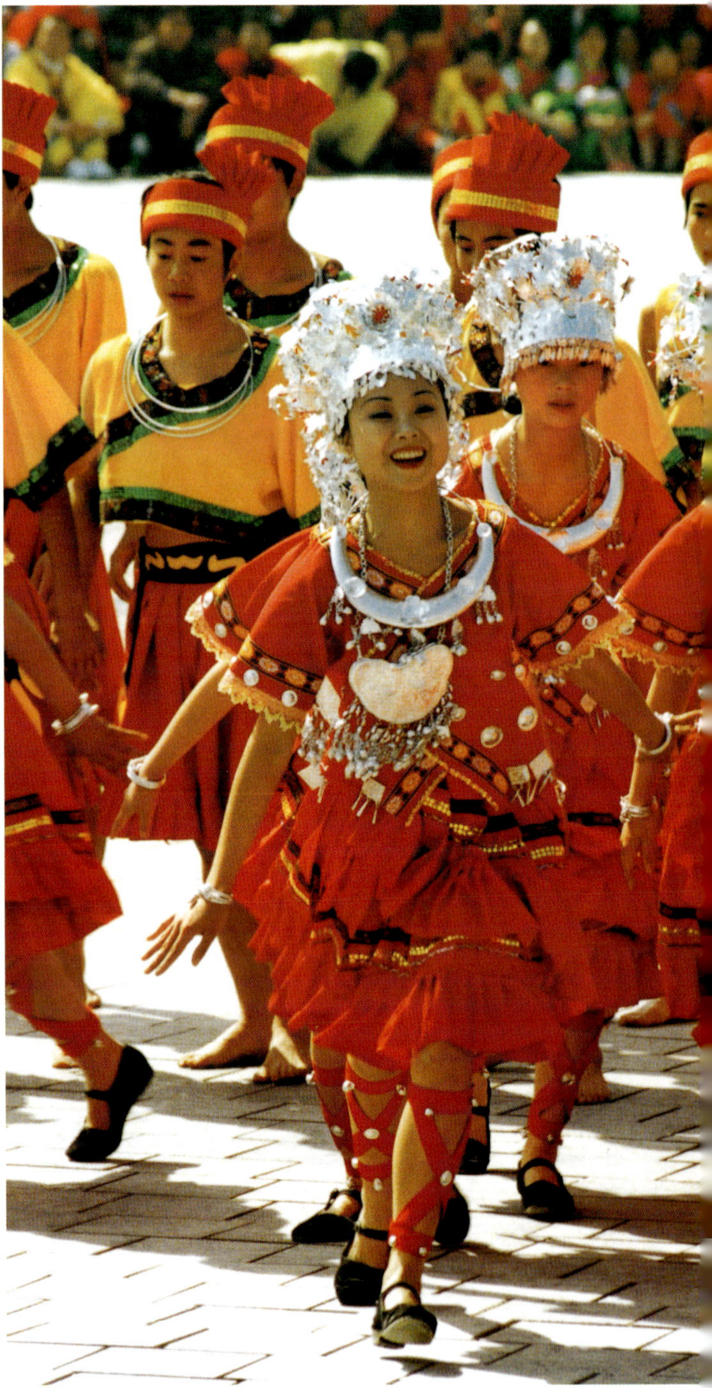

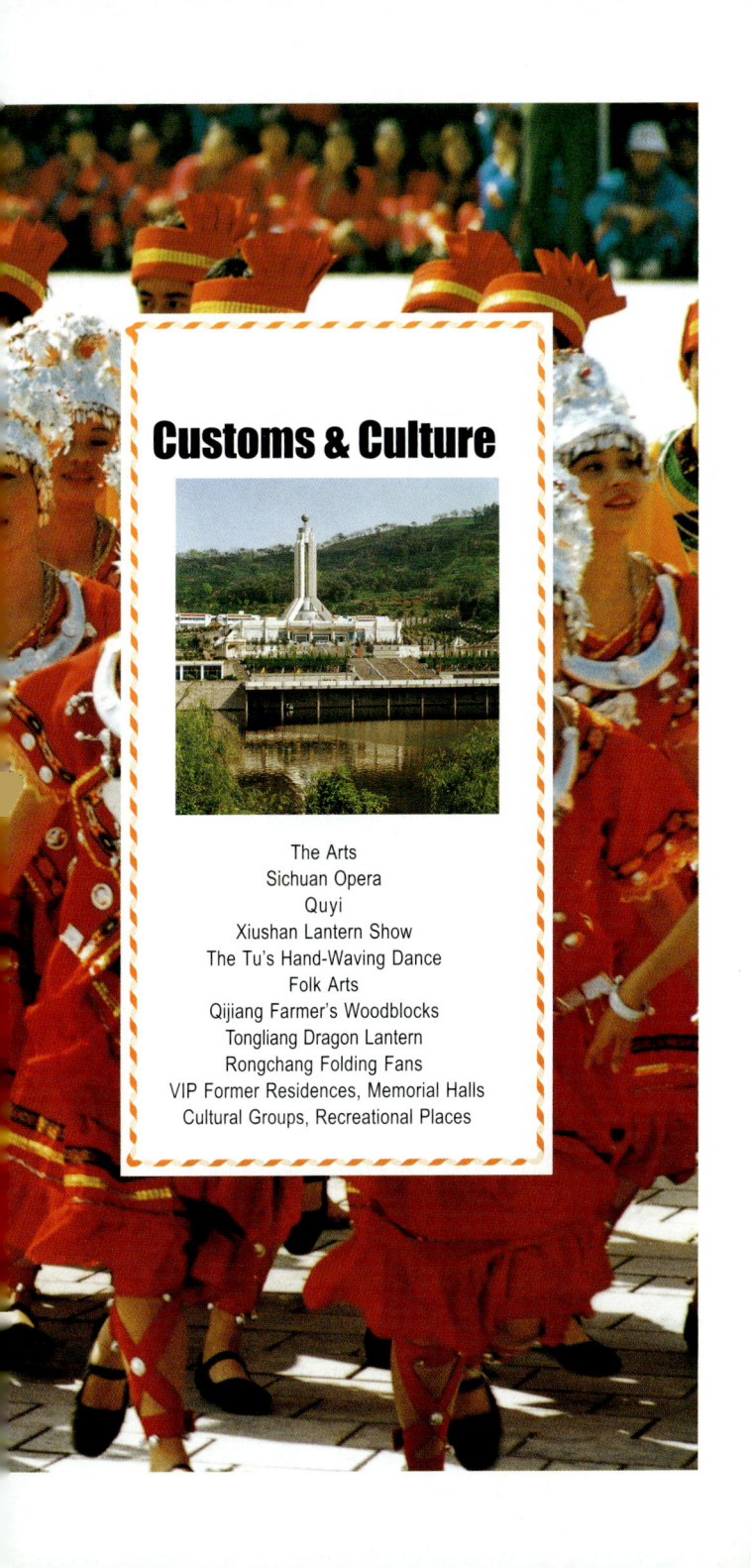

Customs & Culture

The Arts
Sichuan Opera
Quyi
Xiushan Lantern Show
The Tu's Hand-Waving Dance
Folk Arts
Qijiang Farmer's Woodblocks
Tongliang Dragon Lantern
Rongchang Folding Fans
VIP Former Residences, Memorial Halls
Cultural Groups, Recreational Places

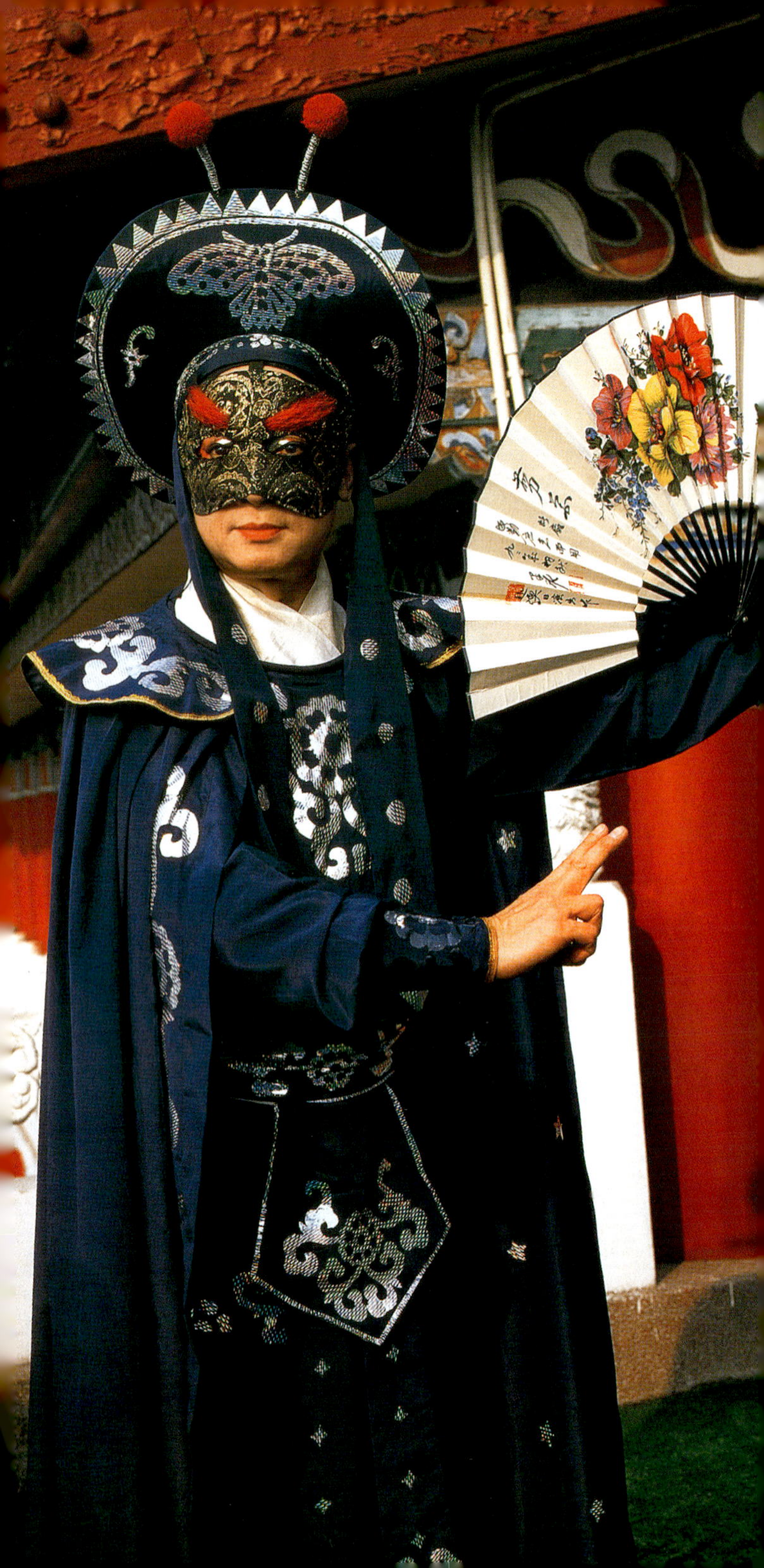

Customs & Culture

The Arts

Sichuan Opera

Sichuan Opera is Chongqing's main local opera, with a history of 300 years. Sichuan Opera is popular in Chongqing, Sichuan, and some areas of Yunnan and Guizhou.

Sichuan Opera includes five reading or singing tunes with Sichuan dialects, i.e. Melodies for Kunqu Opera, loud tune, fiddle, story-telling, and lantern dance. Among them, loud tune has many names, and its melody is charming and moving. It is Sichuan Opera's main singing form. The chorus of Sichuan Opera includes the forms of leading chorus, mixed chorus, vocal accompaniment and an ensemble of two or more singers. The singing is meaningful and thought-provoking. The words used in Sichuan Opera are vivid with a sense of humor, and are full of simple flavor of local life. The art of performance seriously follows styled movements, emphasizes on dance modeling, martial art's skills, and an exquisite performance. Musical instruments are mainly drum-like percussion instruments, i.e. three-tenth singing and seven-tenth percussion, and half play of drum and half play of song. Most of the subjects are collected from classics, fairy tales and legends. Plays are mostly comic. Whatever the plays are—formal, tragic, big, or small—they have more or less comic senses.

Quyi

Folk arts include dulcimer, ballad singing, gold clapper talks, bamboo violin, cart lantern, drum dance, comic play, plate, lotus leaf, a chain of bamboo flutes, story-telling with accompaniment of *pipa*, monologue story-telling with gestures, cross-talk, *kuaiban*, and reading aloud poems with local dialects and stories. The folk arts feature a strong local, cultural flavor, in integrating Sichuan dialects with folk music, telling stories by talking and dancing with movements. Folk arts are performed to portrait figures, express feelings, and reflect real lives.

Folk arts is part of the culture of the local residents for its unmatched advantages. The programs of folk arts are usually short, flexible in forms, vivid, and enthusiastic. Costumes and stage properties are simple and free from the limitation of stage and time.

Xiushan Lantern Show

Xiushan County has long been known as Home of Lantern Dance. Originated from Han people's lantern dance, it consists of the performing skills of the Tujia and Miao peoples, and develops into a new form of art with new styles and

Face Changing

Face changing is a kind of attractive performance skill on stage. It includes some swift postures, such as tearing off, crumpling, and blowing.

Performing Sichuan Opera in a teahouse at Ciqikou.

Xiushan lantern show.

Lantern Performance in the First Lunar Month

Xiushan lantern show is mainly performed during the Spring Festival. On the first day of the First Lunar Month, the lantern show troupe begins performing after worshipping the Lantern God in the Lantern Hall. From the 3rd to 15th days, hundreds of troupes will light lanterns and play gongs and drums to welcome the New Year in villages. Most common lyrics include "lantern watching", "congratulations," "open the gate of fortune", and "thank you, our lord". On the 15th day, the lantern troupes hold a ceremony, burning lanterns, putting an end to the show.

moving singing and dancing, which is now popular among the Han, Tu, and Miao peoples.

Lantern dance doesn't have to be big in group.

There are three forms of lantern dance, including single, double, and colorful. The Single is performed by one female dancer and a clown. The female role is always played by a boy posing as a girl, being tied with crepe hair, wearing colorful skirt, and short clothes, with a silk folding fan in the right hand and a colorful towel in the left hand. The clown is called a beggar, wearing a fur-lined jacket with inside out and a belt, a skullcap or a towel in his left hand, and a big cattail leaf fan in his right hand. The couple has two female representatives and two or four clowns. Lantern dance is somewhat similar with Hunan's drum dance, and has more complete plots.

There are over 200 lantern dances. Dances are played on a mini stage, a square table. It usually begins with a beggar, who finds excuses to invite the leading female onto the stage. They then start to turn around, singing and dancing, with exquisite, precise, and comic performance.

The libretto is short but vigorous, reflecting people's daily lives, love and marriage, working and productive knowledge, and historical and local stories.

There are over 400 names. The lyric is usually simple, five or seven words in a sentence, and two or four sentences in a phrase.

Hand-Waving Song

It is an epic consisting of four parts. The first three parts sing praises to the creation of the world, the immigration of the Tujia people, and agricultural production, while the fourth part is poems. It takes an important position in the Tujia literature.

A hand-waving dance.

The Tu's Hand-Waving Dance

The Baishou, or Hand-Waving, dance is very popular among the Tujia people on festive occasions, such as worshipping to ancestors and praying for good harvests during the 3rd to the 15th days of the first month on lunar calendar, or in the early spring, during which time the Tujias, young and old, dress in *xilankapu*, or quilt cover, carrying banners with phoenix patterns, and shouldering birding pieces and spears, and gather in an open air. A wizard conducts the dance with a tall paper hat, a skirt of thin silk, and a broadsword in his hand with jingle bells. People dance to the accompaniment of drums and guns, and ox horns. The dance consists of two forms, the big and small. The big is mostly for grand ceremonies to worship ancestors, which is held once every three or five years with hundreds of thousands of participants. The small is for ordinary celebrations, usually participated by tens, or hundreds of people. The dance varies in movements, some resembling sacrificial ceremonies, labor, and fights, others hunting, fishing, mountaineering, and crossing rivers.

Woodblock by Qijiang Farmers

The woodblock by farmers in Qijiang is simple yet full of passion. It combines the techniques of traditional Chinese folk art, and refreshes with its own style, depicting legends and their rural life.

Folk Arts

Qijiang Farmer's Woodblocks

Over the last ten years since the popularity of woodblock, more and more farmers in Qijiang County have become enthusiastic in artistic creation. Since 1983, they have created more than 1,000 woodblocks, which were showcased in the China Art Gallery in Beijing in January 1984. Since then, 847 woodblocks by the farmers in Qijiang have been displayed in China as well as more than ten countries and regions, including the US, Japan, Britain, Canada, and Italy. Some 600 works have been collected by national museums or private collectors, and 50 of them have won prizes by the state or the local governments. These works of art, an exotic flower of traditional Chinese folk art, has been highly praised by the art circles at home and abroad. In 1985, Qijiang County was cited as Home of Farmer's Woodblock by the Cultural Department of Sichuan, the Sichuan Artists' Association, and the Chongqing Municipal Government. In February 1988, the Ministry of Culture honored the county as Hometown of Farmer's Paintings in Modern China.

An old artisan.

Handiwork for dragon lanterns.

Tongliang Dragon Lantern

The earliest Tongliang Dragon was found in the Ming Dynasty, and became popular in the Qing Dynasty. The very first dragon, the fire one, was made of ropes and bamboo. Fire-crackers, sometimes lanterns, decorated

Weaving up a dragon.

A game for brave challengers.

the dragon when people played. The fire dragon did not look real without the body and the "flesh." Its big head and long neck were woven with bamboo. However, the dragon dance formed a magnificent view at night. Later, people pasted paper onto the body of the dragon, with lanterns inside. The paper body was painted with bones and shells, more vivid than before.

Over the last few decades, people have tried various ways to improve the dragon by decorating it with the parts of animals. The dragon's mouth, supposed to shut, now opens. The newly-designed dragon is big, long, and vigorous. The shape of the dragon is exaggerated. The body of the dragon, joined with 24 properly-proportioned parts, is more convenient for the players. In recent years, toys and ornaments resembling the dragon have been produced.

At the celebrations of the 35th and 50th anniversaries of the founding of the People's Republic of China in Beijing, nine Tongliang dragons hovered on Tian'anmen Square, arousing great attention from the viewers. The Tongliang dragon dance won the contest of dragon dances to celebrate the Visit Beijing '98.

Rongchang Folding Fans

Folding fans are practical in use in summer, a work of art, and an important property in operas and dancing.

The folding fans were introduced from Korea in the Northern Song Dynasty.

The production of folding fans in Rongchang began in 1551, the 30th year of Emperor Jiajing's reign of the Ming Dynasty. The fans enjoyed high reputation for its fine quality and elegant appearance.

The folding fans of Rongchang are meticulous in craftsmanship. It can be used in daily life and serves as a rare work of arts and crafts. Since ancient times, folding fans made in Rongchang have been sold well in China, and in other countries, such as India and Myanmar. Over the last few decades, Rongchang has seen a rapid development in the production of folding fans by diversifying the variety of the products, 345 in total. The folding fans with paintings are especially accepted by the departments of tourism and the arts.

Craftsmanship of Folding Fans

A folding fan consists of two parts, the ribs and the covering. The material for the ribs can be bamboo, sanders, wood, and bones, while that for the covering paper and silk. The production of folding fans contains 145 steps, which requires even and proper connection of each step.

Customs & Culture

VIP Former Residences, Memorial Halls

Former Residence of Soong Ching-ling

Located at 5 New Village on Lianglukou Road, Yuzhong District, the Former Residence of Soong Ching-ling consists of wood-and-brick structures, including the main building, the rear building, and air-raid shelter. On display in the rooms are 110 articles and photos when Soong stayed in Chongqing during 1942 and 1945, showcasing her outstanding contributions to the reestablishment of the United League of China organized by Dr. Sun Yat-sen in 1905, which became the Chinese Nationalist Party in 1912, her endeavor in the cooperation of the CPC and KMT, her efforts in winning international support, and her devotion to the triumph of the Anti-Japanese War through material transportation, aid of the wounded, and concern for orphans and refugees.

Former Residence of Liu Bocheng

A relic under municipal protection, the former residence of Liu Bocheng is a one-story compound house located in Zhaojia Town, 28 kilometers south of Kaixian County, and 56 kilometers from Wanzhou City. The rooms where Liu was born and studied are well preserved. In front of the house there are elegant sculptures and two big trees. The year 1989 saw the restoration of the house, with exhibition rooms and receptions.

Former Residence of Nie Rongzhen

Also known as Shiyuanzi, the former residence of Nie Rongzhen is located in Langjia Village of Wutan Town, Jiangjin City. It faces east, and has 17 rooms. Nie spent his childhood here. In 1914, the Nie's moved elsewhere nearby. Five years later, Nie Rongzhen went to France for further study while taking a part-time job; and he never returned to his

Soong Ching-ling (1893-1981)

Soong Ching-ling, the wife of Dr. Sun Yat-sen, is one of the leaders of the People's Republic of China. A native of Wenchang, Hainan Province, Madam Soong was born in Shanghai.

During the Anti-Japanese War, Madam Soong devoted painstaking efforts in supporting the CPC. In May 1981, she became a CPC member, and was made honorary president of China at the 5th Session of the National People's Congress. She died of illness on May 29, 1981.

The Memorial Hall to Liu Bocheng.

Liu Bocheng (1892-1986)

A native of Kaixian County, Liu Bocheng began his revolutionary career at the age of 19, and served as chief of staff of the Red Army, commander of the 129 Division, and commander of the 2nd Field Army. He is one of the ten great marshals of China, and a great revolutionary and strategist. Liu died of illness in October 1986. On October 24, 1986, Liu's remains were sent back to Kaixian and scattered around the sculptures in front of his former residence.

The Memorial Hall to Nie Rongzhen is now a state Grade AAAA tourist attraction.

Nie Rongzhen (1899-1992)

A native of Jiangjin, Nie Rongzhen is one of the ten great marshals and a great revolutionary and strategist. In 1919, he went to France for further study while taking a part-time job. In 1924, he went to Moscow for further study. In 1927, he led the Nanchang and Guangzhou uprisings. After the founding of the People's Republic, he worked as mayor of Beijing, chief of staff of the People's Liberation Army, vice-premier of the State Council, member of the Political Bureau of the CPC Committee, vice-president of the Central Military Committee, and vice-president of the Standing Committee of the National People's Congress.

Residence in the ancient town of Shuangjiang.

Zhao Shiyan (1901-1927)

A native of Youyang County, Zhao Shiyan is a revolutionary and one of the leaders of three workers' uprisings in Shanghai. In 1914, Zhao went to Beiping, Beijing today, to study, and became one of the CPC leaders. He was arrested by the KMT on July 2, 1927 in Shanghai and was murdered 17 days later.

hometown. In 1989, the residence was rebuilt after the original model.

Five rooms in the residence are furnished with the original furniture, and the rest rooms work as exhibition halls, displaying 35 articles used by young Nie, which include clothes, toys, books, inkstone, brush pot, paintings, academic records, and letters.

Former Residence of Yang Yingong

Located in Shuangjiang Town, 10 kilometers northwest of Tongnan County, it is also the former resident of Yang Shangkun, former president of China. Covering 1,600 square meters in area, it is a structure built in the late Qing Dynasty, with well-preserved grey tiles, white walls, black beams, and front gate.

In 1927, Yang Yingong, brother of Yang Shangkun, died in the March 31 Incident at the age of 29, when he served as Party secretary of the Chongqing Committee. Under his guidance and influence, the Yang's brothers and sisters, including Hengshi, Shangkun, Baibing, Shanghua, Yijun, and Bailin, joined the Communist Party and devoted themselves to the Chinese revolution at young age. On display are the diary of Yang Yingong, relics, and photos.

Cemetery of Yang Yingong and Yang Shangkun

The Cemetery, a relic under major municipal protection, is located one kilometer southeast of Shuangjiang Town. In the middle of the tomb there is an archway. A red marble statue of Yang Yingong stands in the cemetery with lush trees and flowers blossoming all year round.

In 2001, a cemetery of Yang Shangkun was established next to the Cemetery of Yang Yingong. There are a red marble statue of Yang Shangkun, a square, and stairs leading to the tomb.

Former Residence of Zhao Shiyan

Located in Longtan Town, Youyang County, the former residence of Zhao Shiyan covers an area of 1,605 square meters, with a floor space of 710 square meters. It is a one-story compound house built with bricks and wood after the model of the Qing Dynasty, and has 32 rooms. The gate faces east, and the rooms face south. The first room in the east used to be Zhao's bedroom. The horizontal board over the gate of the residence was inscribed by Deng Xiaoping. In front of the house stands a statue of Zhao Shiyan. There are two courtyards, one front, another rear. On the wall by the front gate there is a relief of pines and cranes.

Former Residence and Tomb of Chen Duxiu

The former residence of Chen Duxiu is located in Heshanping, 15 kilometers from downtown Jiangjin. It used to be the residence of Yang Shiqin, palace graduate of the Qing Dynasty. There are six Qing-style structures in the courtyard. The eastern-wing house was Chen's bedroom. Many VIPs of the CPC and KMT, including Zhou Enlai, Dong Biwu, Hu Zongnan, and Dai Li, came to visit Chen. The former study of Chen Duxiu now serves as an exhibition room for relics.

Chen Duxiu (1880-1942)

Also known as Zhongpu, Chen Duxiu is a native of Huaining, Anhui Province, a backbone force of the May 4th Movement, and one of the founders of the CPC. He studied in Japan when he was young. In 1920, he proposed the organization of the CPC group in Shanghai. In 1921 when the CPC was founded, he was made general secretary. He stayed in Jiangjin in August 1938, and died of illness on May 27, 1942.

Former Residence of Joseph Warren Stiwell

Located at 63 Jialing New Village in the Yuzhong District, the Former Residence of Joseph Warren Stiwell is a relic under municipal protection, and is now a museum, which consists of the exhibition halls of General Joseph Warren Stiwell, Flying Tiger, Hump Flight, Yan'an Observation Group, and the Sino-American Relationship during the War.

Joseph Warren Stiwell (1883-1946)

A well-known American general, he fought in World War I and served for 13 years in China, beginning in 1942, as commander of U.S. troops in China-Myanmar-India area and chief of staff of Chiang Kai-shek to back up the Chinese people against Japanese invasion. General Joseph Warren Stiwell insisted on the joint efforts to fight against Japanese invasion and became a good friend of the Chinese people.

Memorial Hall to Qiu Shaoyun

Standing on top of Mt. Fengshan in Ximen, Tongliang County, the memorial hall occupies 16 square kilometers in area. Qiu Shaoyun was born in 1931 in Tongliang County. On display are the story of martyr Qiu Shaoyun, more than 200 relics, and a monument inscribed by General Commander Zhu De.

Qiu Shaoyun (1931-1952)

A native of Tongliang, Qiu Shaoyun joined the People's Liberation Army in 1949 and the Chinese People's Volunteers in 1951. Qiu was unfortunately burnt to death during a frontier fight in Korea on October 12, 1952, becoming a national hero followed by many others.

Cultural Groups, Recreational Places

Relieves of the Han Dynasty

In 1953, eight pieces of stone relief were unearthed from a stone tomb of the Han Dynasty. The longest measures 798 centimeters long, consisting of six pieces of stones, and the other two measured 318 centimeters long. The six-piece stone relief have carvings of 83 figures, 12 charts, 56 horses, and one rabbit, while the two-piece stone relief a kitchen, a dining hall, and a big banquet hall with singers and dancers.

Chongqing Museum of Nature & History

Opening hours: 9:00~17:00

A stone relief of the Han Dynasty.

Chongqing Museum of Nature & History

Located on Zhengjie of Mt. Pipa, Yuzhong District, the museum has a collection of more than 120,000 relics and samples, quite a number of which are state Class I and II relics. On display are boats of the Ba people in ancient times, images of the Han Dynasty, and paintings and calligraphy since the Song Dynasty, in addition to currencies of past dynasties, bounded books, relics of the ethnic groups, pottery and porcelain ware since the primitive society, and fossils of ancient living creatures discovered in Yongchuan and Zigong. The four-story museum has 40 exhibition rooms, big enough to hold 500 visitors.

The branch of the Chongqing Museum of Nature & History is located in Wenxingwang, Beibei District, with an area of 20,000 square meters. The predecessor of the museum was known as the China West Museum, founded in 1943 by Mr. Lu Zuofu, a patriotic industrialist. It mainly displays fossils and samples of rare species of animals and birds in Sichuan and the rest of Southwest China.

Traditional Chinese Medicine Museum

Located at 101 Zhengjie of Mt. Pipa, Yuzhong District, the museum features the history, medicine, and pharmaceutical of traditional Chinese medicine. A building of traditional Chinese and Western styles, it consists of the halls to showcase ancient books on Chinese medicine, prescriptions, and samples of medicinal herbs, as well as the means of the preparation of Chinese medicine. The museum also collects 3,000 relics founded in the Banpo Cultural Village, and books, tools, and photos of Chinese medicine preparation.

Tongliang Museum

Located in Bachuan Town in central Tongliang County, the museum has a collection of some 10,000 relics in its exhibition halls, including China's No. One Art Gallery, the Culture and Arts of the Dragon, the Elite of Relics, and Calligraphy, Paintings, and Handicrafts. The museum displays the local customs of Tongliang during the Qing Dynasty and the period of the Republic of China with its collection of 500 wooden horizontal boards; the origin and evolution of dragons, and dragon lanterns from all parts of the country; bronze square pots made during the Shang Dynasty, currency during the Warring States Period and the Qing Dynasty; terra-cotta ware of the Ming Dynasty; porcelain ware of the Ming and Qing Dynasties; and works by well-known Chinese artists.

China's No. One Art Gallery

There are 500 wooden horizontal boards made between the Qing Dynasty and the period of the Republic of China in the People's Warehouse of Pingtan Town.

Chongqing Academy of Chinese Painting

The Chongqing Academy of Chinese Painting is an academic institution specializing in the creation, research, exhibition, and collection of Chinese paintings. It has the honor of visitors of senior government officials, such as Li Peng, Yang Shangkun, Zhang Aiping, and Fang Yi, as well as foreign senior officials, such as Shiro Nakano, former Japanese prime minister.

The Exhibition Hall of the Academy in Kangjiantang, Guanyinyan, Yuzhong District has an exhibition area of 450 square meters with 31 movable walls, 180 meters long and 2.8~3.9 meters tall.

The Chongqing Academy of Chinese Painting provides the original work of Chinese paintings and calligraphy by Chinese artists, and offers services for mounting calligraphy and paintings, making frames for calligraphy and paintings, and making arrangement for exhibitions of calligraphy and paintings.

Chongqing Academy of Chinese Painting

Opening hours: 9:00~17:00.

Chongqing Library

Located at 1 Changjiang Yilu and 93 Zhengjie of Mt. Pipa, Yuzhong District, the Chongqing Library was established in 1947, when known as the State Roosevelt Library to commemorate the victory of the anti-fascist war. It was renamed State Southwest People's Library in 1950 and Chongqing Library in 1987.

The library collects mainly books and periodicals after the period of the Republic of China, as well as documents of the United Nations, and bounded books. It is one of the ten largest libraries in China.

Equipped with updated facilities, the library is under the management of computers; and it has been designated by the Ministry of Culture as a library for microform of documents. The system for microform has offered great convenience for readers.

Chongqing Library
Opening hours: Monday ~ Saturday.

Chongqing Children's Library

Located at 1 Jiaochangkou, Yuzhong District, the Chongqing Children's Library was founded in 1950, when known as the Children's Library of the Southwest People's Library. On June 1, 1964, it was renamed Chongqing Children's Library. It has more than 10 service stations and a branch library in Chongqing, with a total collection of 400,000 books. Its clients include pre-school children, junior and senior school students, educators of teenagers, and parents.

Chongqing Children's Library
Opening hours: 12:00~18:00 from Monday to Friday, 9:30~16:30 on Saturday and Monday.

Chongqing Teenager's Scientific & Cultural Center

The Chongqing Teenager's Scientific & Cultural Center is located at the southern end of the Yangtze River Bridge, and is a large recreational place for the popularization of science and technology and entertainment. It provides more than 10 items for young fun seekers, and serves as an arena for parties and performances.

Opening hours: 9:00~17:00

Chongqing Gymnasium

Located at Lianglukou, Yuzhong District, the Gymnasium was founded in 1954 and completed in February 1955, with an area of 18,000 square meters, and a floor space of 8,704 square meters, big enough to accommodate 4,000 audiences at one time. It is a steel-reinforced-concrete structure, with marble walls and decorations of colorful paintings in traditional Chinese style.

Chongqing Stadium

Located by the Chongqing Gymnasium, it was built in 1951 and was completed in May 1956. Covering an area of 120,000 square meters, it is big enough to hold 45,000 people. As a Grade A sports ground, the stadium serves as an important arena for contest and training as well as a place for grand gatherings. There are standard ground for soccer games and plastic cement track, the gymnastic center, the table-tennis center, the training centers for basketball and volleyball, the swimming pool, the parachute tower built in 1942, and the children's swimming pool.

Chongqing Working People's Cultural Center

Ticket: 2 yuan. Transportation: Take Buses or Trolley Buses No. 401, 402, 205, 610, and 109.

Chongqing Working People's Cultural Center

Located on Zhongshan Road, Yuzhong District, the Chongqing Working People's Cultural Center was first built in 1950 on the site of the Eastern Sichuan Teachers' School and Shizhong Garden, and opened in August 1952. With garden-like environment, it consists of a movie theater, an exhibition hall, a library, a science and technology center, a games center, a cultural conference hall, a music hall, an open-air theater, a sports ground, a swimming pool, and a garden of fish and birds, in addition to a teahouse, a restaurant, and a bar. It is a place for important cultural and recreational activities as well as grand gatherings and festive celebrations.

The turning stars.

Acrobatics.

Chongqing Acrobatic Troupe

Founded in June 1951, the Chongqing Acrobatic Troupe is one of the oldest acrobatic troupes in China, combining eight troupes of acrobatics, magic, and circus.

In 1953, the Chongqing Acrobatic Troupe first put acrobatics on the stage. Two years later, it established a band of traditional Chinese musical instruments, the first of its kind in the acrobatic circles, to accompany the acrobatic performances.

Over the last 50 years since its establishment, the Chongqing Acrobatic Troupe has produced a great number of performances, and demonstrated the essence of this form of traditional Chinese art throughout China and in over 200 cities in 45 countries and regions. It has walked away with many honors and titles of domestic and overseas competitions.

Chongqing Song & Dance Ensemble

Founded in 1956, the Chongqing Song & Dance Ensemble enjoys a high fame in southwestern China. Its performances feature a strong local flavor of Sichuan. Over the last few decades, it has toured all parts of China, including Hong Kong and Macao, and performed in foreign countries, including the United States, Myanmar, Japan, France, former Soviet Union, Singapore, and the Philippines. Some of its performances have awarded national prizes, such as *Burning Festive Torches*, *Red Sun*, and *Ode to the Three Gorges*.

Guotai Movie Theater

Located near the Monument to Liberation, Yuzhong District, Guotai Movie Theater was established in 1937, when known as Guotai Opera Theater. It was renamed Peace Movie Theater in 1953 and Guotain Movie Theater in 1993. The well-equipped movie theater has a dance hall, a mall, a restaurant, and a multifunction hall.

Guotai Movie Theater.

Chongqing Modern Drama Troupe

Also known as Chongqing Art Working Troupe, the Chongqing Modern Drama Troup was established in December 1949. Over the last 50 years, it has created and rewritten a great number of modern dramas, including *Red Crag, News in Chongqing,* and *An American General in Chongqing,* and has staged many famous Chinese and foreign dramas, such as *Thunderstorm, Sunrise, The Man Who Returned in Snowy Midnight, Questions on Russia,* and *Carmen,* many of which have won national prizes.

Chongqing Sichuan Opera Theater

Founded in 1951, the Chongqing Sichuan Opera Theater is a combination of the Shengli Sichuan Opera Troupe, the No. 1 Troupe of the Sichuan Theater, and the Yongchuan Sichuan Opera Troupe. Famous Sichuan Opera performers, including Zhang Decheng, Zhou Mulian, Yuan Yukun, and Xu Qianyun, have served as the head of the theater. Over the last 50 years, the theater has staged many famous Sichuan operas, both classical and modern, and has performed in other countries, such as Poland, Czekh, former East Germany, and Bulgaria. Shen Tiemei, a well-known performer, walked away with the Plum Prize at the 6th National Opera Competition, the highest honor of operas in China.

History of Sichuan Opera

Sichuan Opera was first put on stage in the Ming Dynasty. Yang Sheng'an, a distinguished scholar and poet, made great contributions to the popularization of the opera. It took shape in the mid-Qing Dynasty, and became popular in Sichuan in the late Ming Dynasty. Other local operas have enriched Sichuan Opera with the immigration from Jiangxi, Jiangsu, Anhui, Hubei, Shanxi, and Shaanxi.

Gold, a Sichuan Opera.

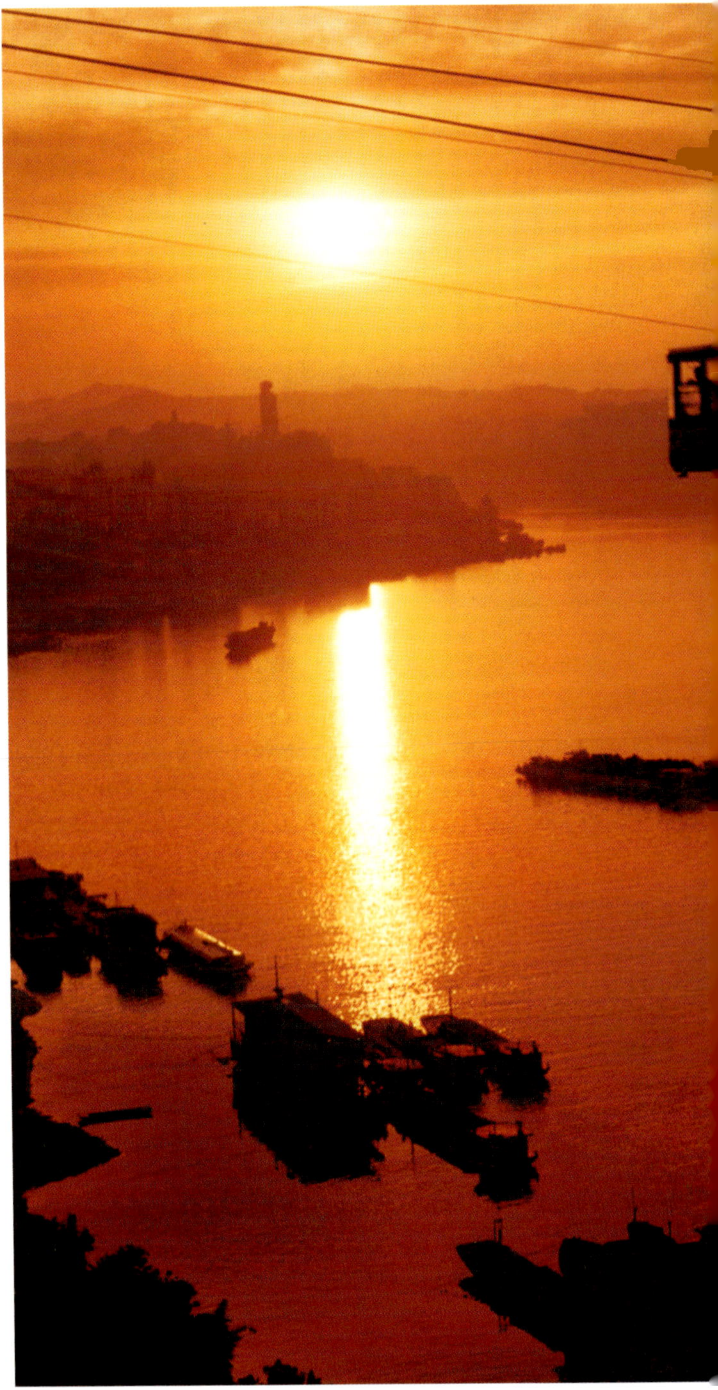

Tourism Information

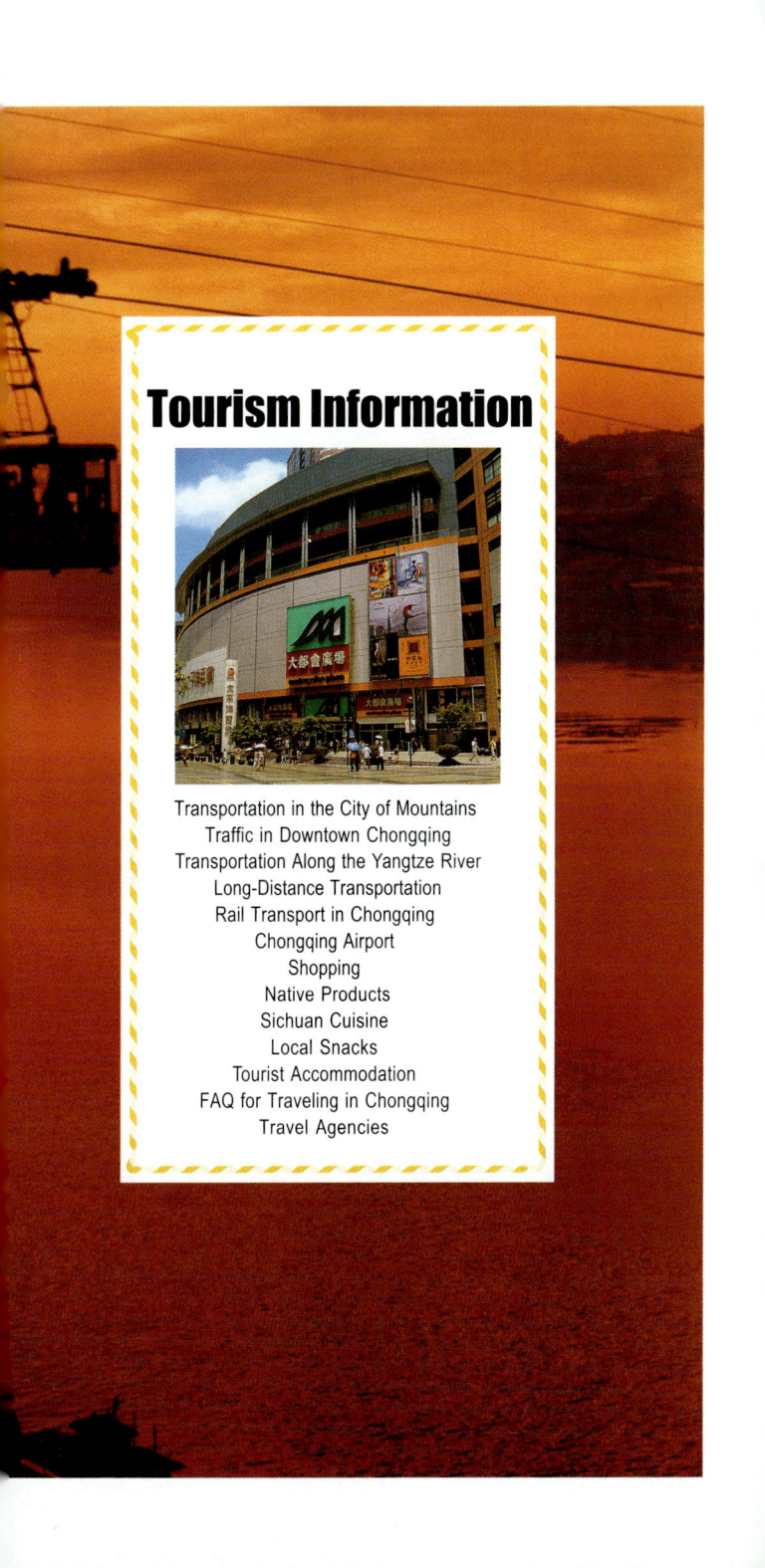

Transportation in the City of Mountains
Traffic in Downtown Chongqing
Transportation Along the Yangtze River
Long-Distance Transportation
Rail Transport in Chongqing
Chongqing Airport
Shopping
Native Products
Sichuan Cuisine
Local Snacks
Tourist Accommodation
FAQ for Traveling in Chongqing
Travel Agencies

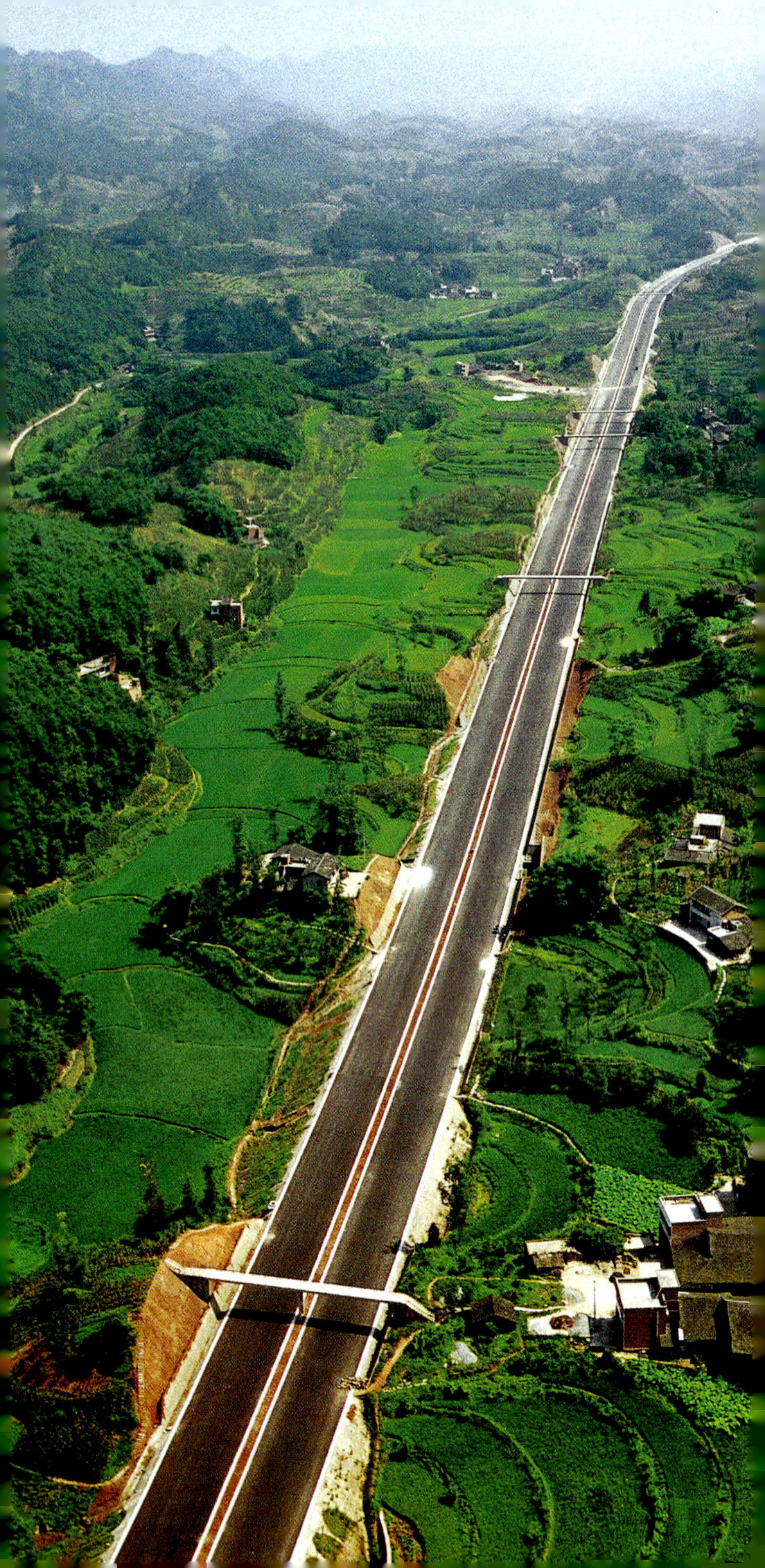

Transportation in the City of Mountains

Chongqing is hemmed in by mountains and rivers. The land forms up and down. Over the last 20 years, the local government has attached special importance to the construction of infrastructural facilities, including the Yangtze River Bridge, the Huanghua Garden Bridge over the Jialing River, the Lijiatuo and Cuntan Bridges over the Yangtze, and highway bridges in Fengdu, Fuling, Zhongxian, Wanzhou, and Jiangjin, 10 in total; the boulevard along the Yangtze and Jialing Rivers; the international airport; the railway stations; and wharves. More than 140 routes have been opened for buses and trolley buses. To suit the special geographical condition, cable ways across the Yangtze and Jialing Rivers, Chaotian Gate, elevators on Caiyuanba and Kaixuan Roads, and in Mt. Gele, have been built.

Chongqing is a hub for water, land, and air transportation in southwest China. Every day, regular flights shuttle between Chongqing and other parts of China, and other countries, such as Thailand, Japan, and South Korea; Cruises of all classes are busy on the rivers of Yangtze, Jialing, and Wujiang; and some 20 trains run between Chongqing and China's major cities, such as Beijing, Shanghai, Guangzhou, Kunming, Chengdu, Xi'an, and Zhengzhou; Vehicles travel along national highways, such as 210, 212, 318, and 319, and expressways, such as Chengdu-Chongqing, and Chengdu-Fuling; Air-conditioned coaches and long-distance buses run between Chongqing and its surrounding areas, such as Chengdu, Yibin, and Leshan.

A cableway over the Yangtze.

A modern overpass in Chongqing.

Huanghuayuan Overpass.

Traffic in Downtown Chongqing

Chongqing has a convenient trans-portation. The main means of transportation are busses and trolleybuses, mostly available from 5:30am through 9:00pm. In recent years, mini vans and air-conditioned buses have been added at peak hours.

Taxi is another means of trans-portation. The earliest taxi in Chongqing was in service in the early 1930s. Ordinary people could hardly afford because it was too expensive. Taxi became popular in the 1980s. The native brand is Lingyang, big enough to hold four people. The least price is 5.00 yuan. An extra 1.20 yuan is added per kilometer. There are also other brands, such as Xiali and Santana, the price of which are 1.40 yuan/km and 1.60 yuan/km respectively. The clients have to pay for toll gates on expressways, 10 yuan. An extra of 0.60 yuan will be charged per five minutes for waiting.

The Crown Elevator

The Crown Elevator was built with a total of 150 million yuan by the Crown Enterprise Co., Ltd., a Sino-foreign joint venture.

Put into operation in 1996, the elevator is 112 meters long, the longest of its kind in Asia, 52.7 meters high, and with a slope of 30 degrees. Every hour, the elevator can carry 130,000 people. It works during 7:00am and 9:00pm.

The transportation network in Chongqing.

Cables & Elevators in Downtown Chongqing

Name	Length (m)	Business hours	Price (yuan)
Yangtze Cableway	1,166	6:30~21:00	1.50
Jialing Cableway	740	6:30~21:00	1.20
Kaixuan Road Elevator	35	6:30~21:00	0.50
Crown Elevator	112	7:00~21:00	1.00

Buses & Trolley Buses

Trolley Buses

401 Shangqingsi-Chaotianmen
402 Jiefangbei-Shapingba
403 Lianglukou-Yangjiaping
404 Yangjiaping-Huochezhan
405 Guanyinqiao-Jiefangbei

Buses

101 Hongqihegou-Shanghengjie
102 Caiyuanba-Chaotianmen
103 Shanqingsi-Chaotianmen
104 Hongyancun-Xiaoshizi
105 Wuyilu-Wuyilu
106 Hongqihegou-Mao'ershi
107 Hongqihegou-Cuntan
108 Nanping-Wulidian
109 Jiaochangkou-Chenjiaping
110 Jianxinbeilu-Yudaishan
111 Wulidian-Xiaoshizi
112 Hongqihegou-Xiaoshizi
113 Jianxinbeilu-Chenjiawan
114 Liangtuoshuichang-Lianglukou
115 Xiji-Dashiba
116 Hongyancun-Huangnibang
117 Guanyinqiao-Wangjiangchang
118 Hongqihegou-Shiqiaopu
120 Chaotianmen-Huayuanxincun
121 Wulidian-Huayuanxincun
122 Niujiaotuo-Niujiaotuo
123 Guanyinqiao-Qingcaoba
128 Waitan-Waitan
125 Nanping-Jiazhouhuayuan
105 Caiyuanba-Caiyuanba
212 Shapingba-Geleshan
213 Shiyuan-Zhongliangshan
214 Shapingba-Dashiba
215 Xiaoshizi-Shuangbei
216 Niujiaotuo-Huochebeizhan
217 Niujiaotuo-Shuangbei
218 Shiyuan-Zhangjiawan
219 Niujiaotuo-Xinqiao
220 Tongjiaqiao-Tuwan
221 Shapingba-Shuangbei

222 Shiqiaopu-Zhongliangshan
223 Yangjiaping-Jiulongpo
224 Jiugongmiao-Chaotianmen
225 Daping-Funiuxi
226 Zhigangdadao-Jiugongmiao
227 Shapingba-Banbianjie
228 Shapingba-Hongcaofang
229 Xijiaogongyuan-Tiaodeng
230 Shapingba-Shizishan
232 Baihuacun-Caiyuanba
233 Yangjiaping-Lijiatuo
301 Wuyilu-Lijiatuo
302 Wuyilu-Jieshi
303 Wuyilu-Yudong
304 Nanping-Danzishi
306 Nanping-Jiaochangkou
309 Lijiatuo-Gongping
310 Yudong-Yangjiaping
310 Daojiao-Chenjiaping
361 Longzhizhong-Jiaochangkou
362 Nanping-Dongwuyuan
363 Danzishi-Lianglukou
365 Liuxiaoqu-Chenjiaping
381 Nanping-Tongyuanju
382 Wugongli-Chaotianmen
383 Wuyilu-Laochang
384 Shangxinjie-Nanshan
384 Shangxinjie-Laochang
392 Chenjiaping-Zhangjiawan
392 Chenjiaping-Huayan
392 Chenjiaping-Erzhoucheng
404 Zhigangdadao-Hanyulu (AC)
405 Longhuahuayuan-Jiefangbei (AC)
412 Guanyinqiao-Maoxiangou
413 Yangjiaping-Chaotianmen
413 Yangjiaping-Jiefangbei (AC)
413 Yangjiaping-Jiefangbei
416 Guanyinqiao-Mawangping
418 Chaotianmen-Huochebeizhan
419 Dayan-Caiyuanba
421 Shipingqiao-Guanyinqiao
429 Shiqiaopu-Jiaochangkou
501 Beibei-Chaotianmen
502 Beibei-Niujiaotuo (AC)

502 Beibei-Chaotianmen
503 Beibei-Caiyuanba
504 Beibei-Shapingba
505 Beibei-Yangjiaping
515 Beibei-Xiema
518 Beibei-Chengjiang
520 Beibei-Jinyunshan
538 Beibei-Niujiaotuo
601 Hongqihegou-Jiefangbei
602 Dianzixiao-Chaotianmen
604 Hongqihegou-Liujiatai
605 Nanqiaosi-Lianglukou
606 Renhe-Caiyuanba
611 Huangnibang-Nanquan

Mini Buses

101 Hongqihegou-Shanghengjie
108 Nanping-Wulidian
109 Jiaochangkou-Wulidian
111 Wulidian-Xiaoshizi
113 Guanyinqiao-Shapingba
119 Nanping-Shiqiaopu
122 Zhuyuanxiaoqu-Zhuyuanxiaoqu
181 Wuyilu-Chenjiawan
216 Niujiaotuo-Jianyuan
218 Shiyuan-Zhongliangshan
221 Shapingba-Duijincun
231 Jianyuan-Jiugongmiao
301 Jiefangbei-Lijiatuo
303 Jiefangbei-Dajiangchang (AC)
304 Nanping-Danzishi
305 Shangxinjie-Nanping
372 Liuxiaoqu-Chaotianmen
373 Houpu-Longzhizhong
381 Nanping-Tongyuanju
412 Hongqihegou-Dongwuyuan
413 Chaotianmen-Dongwuyuan
415 Hongqihegou-Chenjiaping
417 Daping-Liudianzi
428 Huayuancun-Yangjiaping
901 Xijichang-Chenjiawan
902 Hongqihegou-Nanping
918 Songshuqiao-Jiugongmiao

The Three Kingdoms at the Chongqing Harbor.

A night view of Chongqing Harbor.

The Passenger Transport Building at Chongqing Harbor.

Transportation Along the Yangtze River

The wharf for passenger transportation is located at Chaotianmen, the junction of the Yangtze and Jialing Ri-vers, at the eastern end of the Yu-zhong District. It is the best starting point for traveling by boat along the Yangtze. Buses available are No. 401, 418, 102, 103, 128, 232, and 382. Mini buses and taxi are also available at night. Travelers'd better make a good choice for the means of transportation along the Yangtze Three Gorges and the scenic spots along the banks. There are three kinds of ships, including Grade A, the best and the most expensive, mainly for foreign visitors; Grade B, which will stop at major scenic spots along the river and the Three Gorges, mainly for domestic visitors; and Grade C, the inexpensive for ordinary visitors.

How to Buy the Cruise Tickets

Get in the ship half an hour ahead of the schedule. Make sure that you are taking the right ship on the right date. Change the ticket into the berth card at the service counter.

If you want to change the date or the route of the trip, get the refund from the ticket reservation two hours prior to the departure. Group tickets should be returned for the refund 24 hours prior to the departure. A fee of 20 percent of the ticket value will be charged. No tickets are refundable beyond the above-mentioned limitations.

Victoria No. 3.

Major Foreign-Oriented Boats along the Yangtze Three Gorges

Company	Name	Star	Capacity (person)
China Int'l Travel Service	President No. 1 (formerly known as President)	Five	150
	President No. 2 (formerly known as Splendid China)	Four	152
	President No. 3 (formerly known as Yellow Crane)	Four	168
	President No. 4 (formerly known as Yangtze River)	Four	170
Victoria Cruise Co.	Victoria No. 1	Four	158
	Victoria No. 2	Four	152
	Victoria No. 3	Four	156
	Victoria No. 5	Four	154
	Victoria Bright Pearl	Four	150
	Victoria Princess	Four	158
	Victoria Angel	Five	148
	Victoria Blue Whale	Five	148
Yangtze Overseas Travel	State Guest No. 1	Three	166
	State Guest No. 2	Three	152
	State Guest No. 3	Three	168
	State Guest No. 5	Three	160
	State Guest No. 6	Three	136
	State Guest No. 7	Three	136
Lihui Cruise Co.	Xianna (formerly known as Royal Princess)	Four	252
	Xianni (formerly known as Royal Princess)	Four	252
	Xianting (formerly known as Royal Princess)	Five	252
Yangtze Overseas Travel	Emperor, Dragon Boat China	Five	204
	Qianlong, Dragon Boat China	Five	178
	Peaceful Lake, Dragon Boat China	Four	164
	Three Kingdoms, Dragon Boat China	Four	152
Domestic Yangtze Navigation	Landscape (13 in total)		350~450
Yangtze Sightseeing Int'l Travel Service	Yangtze Sightseeing (11 in total)		330~630

Sailing Inquiries

China Int'l Travel Service	010-6903 7561	6903 7560
Victoria Cruise Co.	023-6380 4513	
Chongqing Branch, Yangtze Overseas Travel	023-6383 4201	6384 9664
Lihui Cruise Co.	023-6371 2662	6377 5282
Yangtze Cruise Int'l Travel Service	023-6377 5907	6377 5909
Yangtze Landscape Travel Service	023-6377 3251	6384 3457
Yangtze Sightseeing Int'l Travel Service	023-6384 2200	6384 2136, 6384 2138

Four-Day Trip to the New Three Gorges

The boat starts as 8:00pm after travelers enjoy the well-known hot pot in Chongqing. Travelers will stay overnight on the boat.

Day 1:

Arrive at Fengdu at 7:00am and visit Mt. Mingshan, where the Ghost City is located;

Arrive at Fengjie at 4:00pm, visit Baidi Town, the Palace of Everlasting Peace, where Liu Bei, king of the State of Shu, asked Zhuge Liang, his prime minister, to take care of his son before his death, the Stele Forest, with traces of men of letters of the past dynasties, and Kuimen, a pass at the Qutang Gorge, where Li Bai got inspiration for his poem;

At 6:30pm, the trip to the Qutang Gorge, the first of the Three Gorges, starts. On the deck people can admire the magnificent view along the banks.

Arrive at Mt. Wushan at 8:00pm, and stay overnight on the boat.

Day 2:

Take a luxurious pleasure boat to the Lesser Three Gorges, one of China's Top 40 Tourist Attractions, and enjoy the beautiful landscapes of mountains, rivers, and gorges;

Return to the boat at 10:30am and continue the journey to the Wuxia Gorge, while enjoying the sightseeing of Mt. Wushan and Goddess Peak along the banks;

Arrive at the Xiling Gorge at 2:00pm, experiencing the vast, tranquil Yangtze River;

Stop at Maoping Harbor at 4:30pm. Take a bus to Tanzi Hill, 185 meters from the harbor, and enjoy the panorama of the magnificent Three Gorges;

Return to the boat at 9:00pm, and stay overnight on the boat.

Day 3:

Arrive at Yunyang at 8:00am. Visit the new county seat of Yunyang, where the residents from the Three Gorges area resettle because of the construction of the water conservation project, and where the Temple to General Zhang Fei is relocated. Return to the boat at 9:30am;

Arrive at Shibaozhai, one of the Eight Grotesque Structures in the World, at 5:30pm. Enjoy the panoramic view of the splendid Yangtze River. Return to the boat at 6:30pm, and stay overnight on the boat;

Day 4:

Arrive at Chongqing at 12:00, and relax after the travel.

Prices

Grade A (First-Class Cabin)	1,540 yuan/person (round trip)
Grade B (Second-Class Cabin)	1,020 yuan/person (round trip)
Grade C (Third-Class Cabin)	630 yuan/person (round trip)

It includes accommodation, tourist guide service, and tickets of scenic spots but excludes food and tickets for cable cars.

The new Three Gorges.

Price of Sailing Between Chongqing and Mt. Wushan (RMB yuan)

Name	Chongqing	50	80	105	120	140	160	185	220	260	275
Price	50	Changshou	25	65	80	105	115	155	200	225	245
Price	80	35	Fuling	40	50	80	95	125	170	195	215
Price	105	60	40	Fengdu	20	50	70	110	150	185	205
Price	120	75	45	15	Gaozhen	40	60	85	125	165	180
Price	140	100	75	45	35	Zhongxian	30	65	105	140	160
Price	160	115	95	70	60	30	Xituo	40	90	115	135
Price	185	140	120	95	85	60	35	Wanzhou	50	80	100
Price	220	180	155	135	125	100	80	55	Yunyang	55	65
Price	260	215	190	170	160	135	110	80	55	Fengjie	30
Price	275	235	210	190	180	155	130	100	65	30	Wushan

The hydrofoil craft.   *The Oriental Emperor.*

Long-Distance Buses

Chongqing Harbor Yingbin Bus Station at Chaotianmen
Yibin, Nanchong, Zigong, Luzhou, Linshui, Tongjiang, Liangping, Wanzhou, Tongnan, Tongliang, Dianjiang, Pengshui, Qianjiang, Changshou, Fushun, Dazu, Jianyang

Qiansimen Bus Station
Tel: 6373 0418
Youyang, Qianjiang, Pengshui, Leshan, Weiyuan, Zigong, Enshi, Xuanhan, Tongjiang, Nanxi, Bijie, Luzhou, Nanchong, Lezhi, Renshou, Jiangyou, Xishui

Jiefangbei Bus Station
Chengdu, Qianjiang, Wansheng, Nanchong, Xishui, Zigong, Daguan, Beibei, Yubei

Jiefangbei Long-Distance Bus Station at Qingnian Rd.
Yibin, Nanxi, Renshou, Nanchong, Xishui, Zigong, Panzhihua (sleeper)

Shaqu Bus Station at Shapingba
Nanchong, Quxian, Guang'an, Nanchuan, Shehong, Yibin, Luzhou, Leshan

Nanping West Bus Station at Nanping
Luzhou, Zigong, Neijiang, Yibin, Leshan, Zizhong, Dianjiang, Deyang

Kaixuan Rd. Long-Distance Bus Station
Zigong, Yibin, Leshan, Suining, Wusheng, Qianjiang, Wanzhou, Yongchuan, Bishan, Shuangqiao, Dazu, Wansheng, Nanchuan, Luzhou, Hechuan, Tongguanyi, Xipeng, Jiangjin, Shimen, Baishan, Simianshan

Chongqing Bus (Railway) Station
Tel: 6387 3196
Chengdu, Luzhou, Neijiang, Leshan, Zigong, Wanzhou, Dachuan, Nanchong, Mianyang, Yibin, Qianjiang, Guiyang, Xishui. It is a passenger transportation hub of the Chengdu-Chongqing Expressway.

Chongqing North Bus Station at Hongqihegou
Tel: 6785 3898
Linshui, Tongjiang, Shiyong, Dachuan, Liangping, Wanzhou, Zhongxian, Kaixian

Chenjiaping Bus Station at Chenjiaping
Tel: 6861 4524
Xipeng, Dingjia, Bishan, Jiangjin, Yongchuan, Tongliang, Rongchang, Dazu

Chongqing Exchange Market Bus Station
Qijiang, Luzhou, Datong, Wansheng, Guofu, Tianchi, Xikou, Xiaba, Zigong, Yujia, Lexing, Wanzhou

The Chongqing Railway Station at night.

Map of Major Railways

Rail Transport in Chongqing

The Chongqing Railway Station is located at Caiyuanba, Yuzhong District. It is a hub for rail transport in the city. Three main trunk lines in China meet here, including the 463-kilometer-long Chongqing-Nanyang, the 504-kilometer-long Chengdu-Chongqing, and the 915-kilometer-long Xiangfan-Chongqing. These rails link Chongqing with all parts of China.

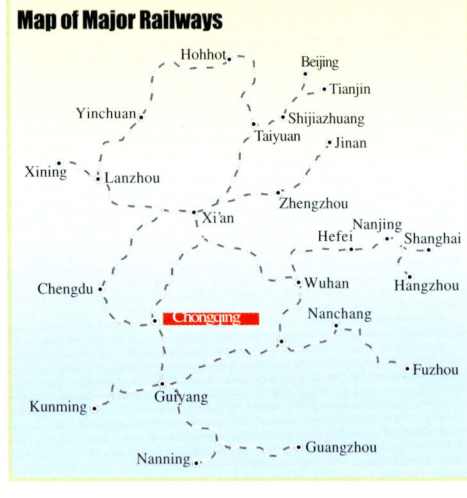

119 Informations touristiques

Jiangbei International Airport, Chongqing.

Chongqing Airport

The Chongqing Jiangbei International Airport is located in the Yubei District, 21 kilometers from downtown Chongqing. It covers an area of three million square meters, with 2,800-meter-long, 60-meter-wide runways. It consists of a lobby, an office building, a weather center, a hotel, and an administration building. Many air companies have offices here, including China Southwest Airlines, Air China, China Southern Airlines, China Eastern Airlines, and China Northern Airlines, as well as Xiamen Airlines Ltd., Sichuan Airlines, Wuhan Airlines, Yunnan Airlines, and Great Wall Airlines. Airplanes, such as Boeing 737, 707, 757, Tu 154, MD-82, and Yu 7, have been put into use. The airport links up 27 large and medium-sized cities in China and Japan, South Korea, and Thailand. With a floor space of 16,000 square meters, the lobby is big enough to hold 1,000 people an hour.

Sketch Map of Major Airlines in Chongqing

Flight to Düsseldorf, Germany

Harbin, Urumqi, Changchun, Shenyang, Hohhot, Beijing, Shijiazhuang, Tianjin, Seoul, Tokyo, Xining, Taiyuan, Jinan, Nagoya, Lanzhou, Zhengzhou, Xi'an, Hefei, Shanghai, Lhasa, Wuhan, Hangzhou, Chengdu, Chongqing, Changsha, Fuzhou, Kunming, Guangzhou, Taipei, Nanning, Shenzhen, Macao, Hong Kong, Haikou, Bangkok

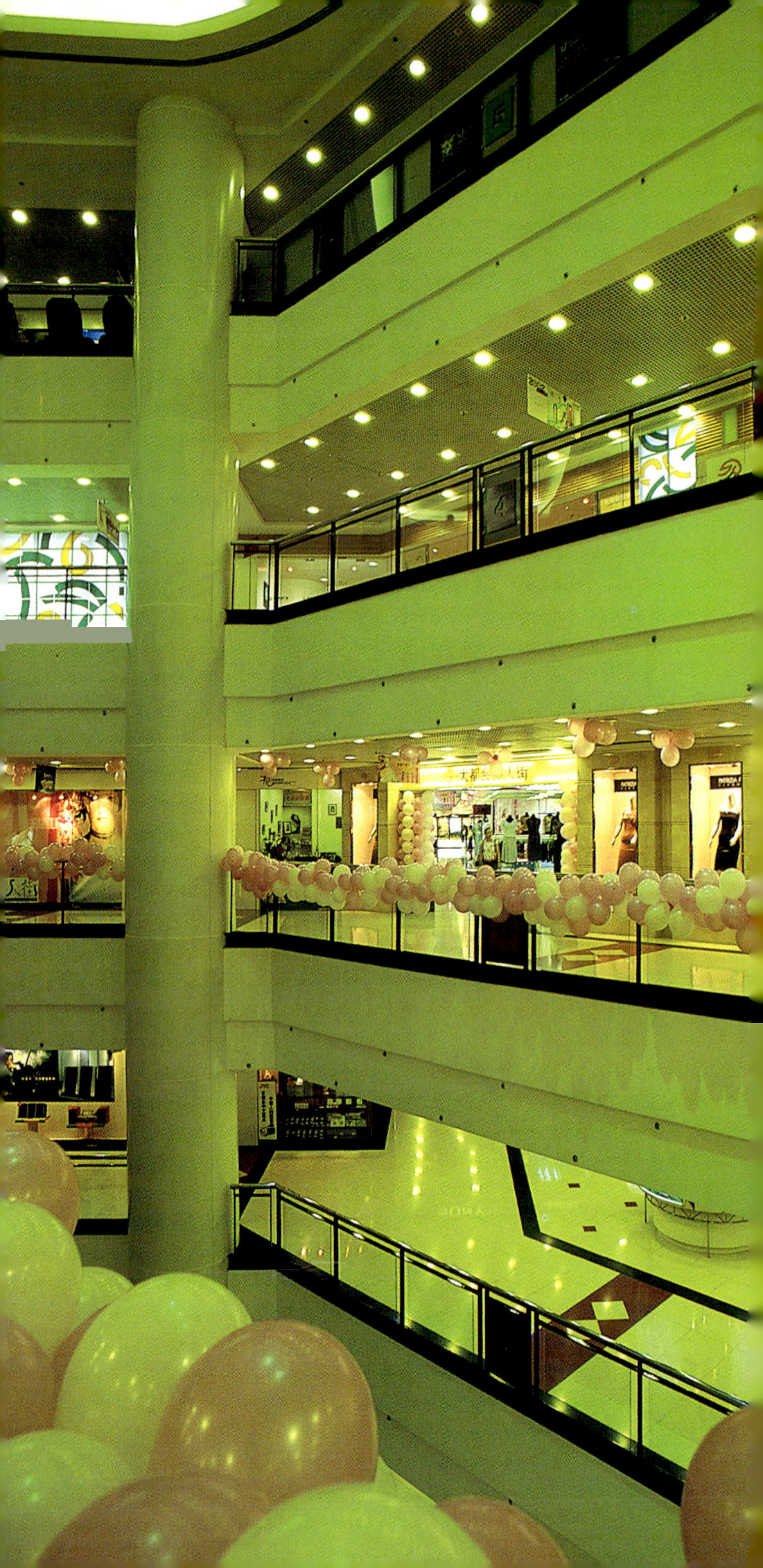

Shopping

With vast land, Chongqing has abundant natural resources and is famous for many local products, thus making the metropolis a shopping paradise. Chongqing is rich in medicinal herbs, including the rhizome of Chinese goldthread and rhizoma gastrodiae from Shizhu, the bark of eucommia from Nanchuan, and miaoshen from Wushan. The geological condition and its climate offer favorable conditions for fruits, such as oranges, pears, shaddocks, and persimmons.

Chongqing is one of the major tea producers in China. The famous brands are Chongqing tuocha, Cuiping yinzhen, and Xinong maojian.

Chongqing is world renowned for snacks, such as dried beef, mustard tuber, and candied rice.

Chongqing is home to Sichuan embroidery, one of the four famous Chinese embroideries, the other three being Jiangsu, Hunan, and Guangdong. Rongchang folding fans has been famous worldwide since the Qing Dynasty. Other local products include the woven bamboo articles, and stoneslabs, the wookblock by farmers in Qijiang, the glassware of Beibei, and porcelain ware from Zhaofeng.

Chongqing Department Store.

Three Gorges Square, Shapingba.

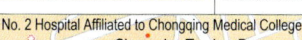

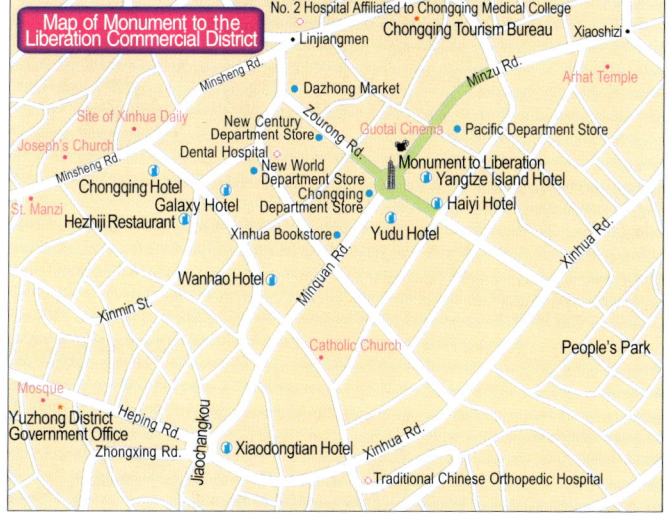

A showcase.

Map of Monument to the Liberation Commercial District

Native Products, Medicinal Herbs

Rhizome of Chinese goldthread
Shizhu County is famous for rhizome of Chinese goldthread, which used to be a tribute to the royal court. It can clear away heat and eliminate dampness, purge intense heat, and remove toxic substances.

Hemp
Shizhu County is famous for hemp, big and round in size, and crystal. It can tranquilize the endogenous wind and arrest convulsion.

Eucommia bark
A native product of Nanchuan, it can tonify the liver and the kidney, reinforce muscles and bones, prevent abortion, and lower blood pressure.

Dangshen
Also known as miaoshen, it is a native product of Mt. Wushan, and can tonify the midde-*jiao*, reinforce *qi*, or vital energy, remove heat from the lung, and dissolve phlegm.

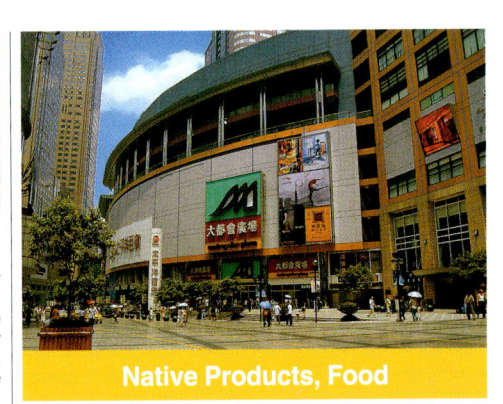

Native Products, Food

Lantern-Shadow Beef
The Lantern-Shadow beef is made by the Old Sichuan Restaurant in Chongqing. Only seven kilograms of meat can be selected from an ox. With Sichuan-flavored ingredients and meticulously made, it tastes fragrant, hot and spicy.

Pickled Dried Meat
A traditional local flavor of Fuling, the pickled dried meat is beautiful in color and fresh in taste. It is another best choice for wine.

Golden-Angle Dried Beef
Famous since 1937, the Golden-Angle brand dried beef is meticulously made with fresh beef and rich ingredients, such as sugar, salt, natural spices, and refined plant oil. It is good for the spleen, stomach, and liver.

Yongchuan-brand Preserved Eggs
Famous some 100 years ago, the Yongchuan-brand preserved eggs contains no lead, with crystal egg white and orange yolk.

Jiangjin Candied Rice
Jiangjin has long been famous for candied rice for over 100 years. The candied rice is made of fine-quality glutinous rice, sugar, plant oil, groundnuts, rose sugar, and sesame. It tastes crispy, pure, and

Tourism Information

fresh, and can nourish *yin*, stimulate one's appetite, and tonify the spleen.

Baishiyi Pressed Duck

With a history of 100 years, the pressed duck is made in Baishiyi Town, Baxian County. It is brown in color, and is the best dish for wine.

Spicy Groundnuts

The Meisheng-brand Hot and Spicy Groundnuts is made of fine-selection of groundnuts, sugar, refined plant oil, and other ingredients. It tastes fragrant, short, sweet, salty, hot, and spicy.

Orange Candy

The orange candy is a traditional local snack in Chongqing. It is white and crystal, fresh and sweet.

Sanjiang-brand Walnuts

Made by the Hechuan Walnut Factory, it has a history of 140 years. The Sanjiang-brand Walnuts is made of fine-quality glutinous rice, sugar, sesame oil, pig fat, walnuts, and roses. It tastes soft, fragrant and sweet, and is good for the kidney and the lung.

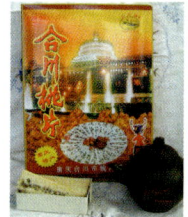

Shunfa-brand Sesame Candy

The Shuanfa-brand Sesame Candy is made by the Jiangjin Shunfa Sesame Candy Plant, which was established some 300 years ago. It is made of pure malt sugar, and tastes fragrant, short, crispy, and sweet.

Candied Groundnuts

A famous local snack in Chongqing, the candied groundnuts is white in color, and tastes sweet, crispy, fragrant, and short.

Sesame Chips

One of the traditional local snacks in Chongqing, the sesame chips shapes in bite-sized square, milky in color, and tastes fragrant, sweet, soft, and crispy.

Baoding-brand Preserved Dried Mustard Greens

The Dazu Yushengtong Distillery was established more than 100 years ago. One of its products known as Baoding is the preserved dried mustard greens, which takes three years to finish. It is appetizing and can be cooked together with pork, fried, boiled, or steamed, and pastries.

Fuling Pickled Mustard

The production of the pickled mustard can be dated back to the reign of Emperor Guangxu of the Qing Dynasty. A time-honored local flavor of Chongqing, it is nutritious and high-up on the menu of the Chinese tables.

The Carrefour.

Ingredients for Hot Pot

Chongqing hot pot has a long history and has long been known at home and abroad. This brand of ingredients is meticulously made and featured by spicy, hot, fresh, and fragrant tastes with carefully selected ingredients, natural and additive and pigment free. It is an ideal choice for hot pot as well as a gift from friends and relatives.

Shancheng-brand Thick Broad-Bean Sauce

Made by the Chongqing Distillery, the Shancheng-brand Thick Broad-Bean Sauce consists of fine-quality broad beans, sesame oil, chilly, and sugar. It is brown in color, and tastes soft, fresh, sweet, salty, and hot.

Flower Root

A famous local snack in Tongliang County, the Flower Root was known as the Orchid Root some 100 years ago. Made in a dozen steps, it is in the shape of silkworm, yellow in color, and fragrant and crispy in taste.

Pepper and Salt Sesame Cake

Also known as Sesame Cake, it is one of the famous pastries in Sichuan. It has thin covering and rich fillings, and tastes sweet, salty, a little bit spicy, and fragrant.

Fish-skin Groundnuts

The skin is short and the nut inside is crispy. The main ingredients include groundnuts, cake flour, and sugar.

Short Candy

The short candy is a common candy in Chongqing. Glutinous rice, sweet potato, sugar, maltose, sesame, and groundnut oil are the main ingredients. It is short and crispy.

Yuenan Bubble Candy

A famous local snack of Chongqing, with a history of 100 years, the Yuenan Bubble Candy is snow white and crystal.

Dragon & Phoenix Cake

The Dragon & Phoenix Cake is a representative of the Sichuan-style pastry, with a history of 600 years. It is fully round with rich patterns of dragon, phoenix, flower, plants, insects, and fish, or with Chinese characters of Happiness or Longevity. It is mostly served at wedding ceremonies or birthday celebrations, and is thus known as the "cake of happiness" of the "cake of longevity."

Chongqing Department Store.

Xiushan Snow Date

Xiushan date features crispiness and fragrance. The main ingredients are glutinous rice, tea oil, and sugar. It is snow white in color, soft, short, sweet and fragrant yet not greasy.

Dragon & Phoenix Candy

The Phoenix-brand candy is a typical candy produced by Changshou County, which has a long history. It is especially served on wedding ceremonies.

Fu'an Department Store.

Yongchuan Fermented Soy Bean

The fermented soy bean is made by the Yongchuan Distillery, which was established 200 years ago. Fine-quality soy bean, glutinous rice, and wine are the main ingredients. It contains rich protein, fat, sugar, amino acid, and vitamin, and is a must ingredient for cooking.

Longevity-brand Meat and Tofu

A traditional local flavor of Changshou (Longevity) County, the dish is salty and fresh, and convenient to serve.

Immortal-brand Fermented Bean Curd

A traditional local flavor in Fengdu County, the Immortal-brand Fermented Bean Curd is bright in color, fine in quality, and fresh and fragrant in taste.

Osmanthus Garlic

The osmanthus garlic is made by the Tongnan Distillery in Chongqing. It is fragrant, sweet, tender and crispy, stimulates one's appetite, and is good for people's health.

Fried Dough Twist

The fried dough twist is shaped like rope, light brown in color, short, crispy, and fragrant in taste.

The pedestrian mall.

Hanguang Department Store

Native Products, Fruits

Red-Robe Orange

A famous species among oranges, it is produced in Wanzhou along the banks of the Yangtze River, Jiangjin, and Baxian County. It is red in color, with thin skin, juicy, and fresh and sweet taste.

Fuling Orange

A local product of Changshou Lake, the Fuling orange is orange red, juicy with less stones, properly sweet and sour, and contains rich sugar, amylaceum, amino acid, and vitamin.

Cangxi Snow Pear

The Cangxi snow pear is in the shape of pebble or gourd, yellow-green-brown in color, and big in size. It tastes crispy and sweet, with rich juice.

Fengjie Navel Orange

Navel orange is the best variety among other oranges. It is beautiful and bright in color, crispy, sweet and sour, stoneless, and easy to skin.

Liangping Shaddock

Produced in Liangping County, with a history of more than 200 years, it is a fine seedling of shaddock. It has thin skin, tender, fragrant, juicy, and nutritious.

Huangsha White Shaddock

Produced in Dianjiang County, it is soft, juicy, and properly sweet and sour.

Changshou Shatian Shaddock

Produced in Changshou County, the Shatian shaddock is fresh, fragrant, and very sweet and juicy. It is in the shape of gourd, and with patterns of the coins in ancient China.

Yangjiao Pear

Produced in Yangjiao of Wulong County, with a history of 250 years, the pear has beautiful shape, juicy, fresh, sweet, and fragrant.

Tourism Information

Chengkou Mopan Persimmon

Chengkou County has a long history of planting persimmon, which is nutritious with rich protein, fat, amylaceum, mannitol, carotene, mineral salt, and vitamin. It is the best fruit for autumn and winter.

Native Products, Tea

Bashan Silver-sprout Tea

The Shiling Tea Plant in Baxian County produces high-quality tea. The Bashan Silver-sprout Tea is straight and tightened, bright in color, and sweet in taste.

Jingxing Green Tea

Produced in Jingxingtai, Wansheng District, the Jingxing Green Tea is strongly fragrant, thick and fresh. The color of the tea is green, and the leaf is tender and green.

Cuiping Silver-needle Tea

The Cuiping Silver-needle Tea is a famous brand in Chongqing. It is fragrant and fresh, thick and refreshing. The tea is crystal clear, and the surface of the leaf is straight and symmetric.

Jinyun Maofeng

The Jinyun Maofeng was developed by the Tea Plant of the Southwest University 20 years ago. The tea leaf has long fine hair, and the tea is fresh and crystal clear.

Yuwu Tea from Mt. Simian

It is made of tea leaves grown 1,000 meters above sea level, and processed in traditional and modern techniques. It looks tender and green, and tastes sweet and fragrant.

Xinong Maojian

A special kind of jasmine tea, it is made of fine-quality tea leaves in early spring and jasmine in summer. The Xinong Maojian is green in color, fresh and sweet in taste, sending forth with fragrance after being infused.

Qianjiang Zhenzhulan Tea

It is a product of a tea manufacturer under the Chongqing Zhenzhulan Tea Company. Made of a fine-quality tea known as Zhenzhulanhua, it tastes thick and fragrant.

The fragrant snow tea from Hongyan, Yuyun.

Native Products, Liquor

Chongqing Beer

This famous brand of Chongqing Beer Brewery is made from fine barley, rice and hops from the Xinjiang Uygur Autonomous Region, which produces its unique brightness, refreshing and full beer foam.

Sixian Taibai Spirit

This famous brand is produced by Wanzhou Taibai Brewery of Chongqing and named after the famous poet of Tang Dynasty, Li Bai (Taibai), a heavy drinker. The spirit is made from rice, glutinous rice, sorghum, barley and corn with 60% of alcohol. The taste of the spirit is mild and sweet. Made by the Wanzhou Taibai Brewery of Chongqing, Sixian Taibai Spirit is a ministerial-level Excellent Product, a winner of a Famous Brand by Sichuan Province for four years running, and a Golden Prize winner of the Second China Food Fair in September 2001.

Dinu Daqu Spirit

This spirit is made in Dazu County which is well known for its good water quality, fine material and excellent technology of brewery. With high percentage of alcohol, this spirit is mild and refreshing, fragrant.

Jijiang Spirit

This spirit is a famous brand of the Jiangjin Brewery of Chongqing. The spirit is brewed from pure sorghum with traditional technology, which create a mild, sweet and fragrant taste.

Fine Brewed Tangerine Wine

This brand of sweet fruit wine is made by the Jiangjin Fruit Wine Brewery of Chongqing. The wine is in bright amber color and tastes mild and full of fruit flavor.

Chinese Kiwi Fruit Wine

Made by Chongqing Tangerine Wine Brewery from selected kiwi fruit, this wine has a flavor of both kiwi and mellow wine. It is bright orange in color, sweet and mild in taste, and nutritious.

Tourism Information

Native Products, Wares

The Tujia brocade.

Sichuan Embroidery

As one of the top four embroideries in China, Sichuan Embroidery is characterized for its dense stitches and smooth surface, with an excellent balance of density and extension. The contents are mainly copies of paintings and photographs.

Xilankapu

Literally means quilt with flower design or brocade of the Tujia People, it is one of the essence of Tujia's fine local arts. When weaving, red, blue and white cotton lines are used vertically, and silk, cotton and wool lines in different colors horizontally. The all hand weaving pieces usually use symmetrical line, simple design, original and elegant, practical and decorative.

A pottery production line in Chongqing.

Sichuan embroidery.

Chongqing Chinaware

The chinaware made by the Zhaofeng Chinaware Manufacture Co. has over 500 kinds, including those for hotels, families, and art chinaware. This product has smooth touch, fine quality, and crisp sound. It is easy to clean and has 2-4 times of service life than ordinary ones. The products have been exported to 40 countries, including the United States, Britain, and Japan, and used in the Great Hall of the People and Diaoyutai State Guest House in Beijing. It used to be a gift when former President Jiang Zemin visited the United States.

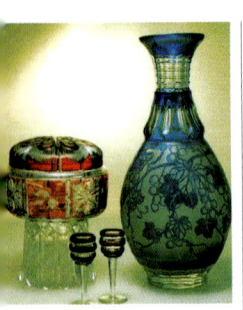

Lotus Glassware

Made by the Chongqing Beibei Glassware Factory, this product are original in design, bright in color, and transparent in view.

Dazu Stone Carvings

The most representative stone carvings made by artisans in Dazu include the statues of Samantabhadra, the Goddess of Water and the Moon, and the Flute Girl. Every year, tens of thousands of such works are made, winning favor from people in Hong Kong, Macao, and Taiwan, and they are exported to dozens of countries, such as the US, Britain, France, Japan, Thailand, and South Korea.

Longshui Hardware

The history of hardware production in Longshui Town, Dazu County, can be dated back to the Tang Dynasty. The knives by Shunfa Knife Factory in Dazu County are made of fine stainless steel, with ox horn and steel for handle. The main products include kitchen knife, fruit knife, and travel knife.

Three Gorges Stone Inkslab

Also known as Xiayan Inkslab, this inkslab is made of Ziyun Stone from Libi Gorges of the Jialing River in Beibei County. The inkslab is made of fine gray stone with exquisite technology and craft. As one of the three famous inkslabs in Sichuan and Chongqing, it is a favorable brand for scholars through hundreds of years.

Mengli Bamboo Weaving

The bamboo weavings made by Jiangjin Bamboo Production Factory include bed cushion, pillow cushion, sofa cushion, car seat cushion, bamboo curtain, and bamboo carpet, all with natural color of bamboo, cool, soft, comfortable and refreshing.

Tongliang Arts & Crafts

Tongliang has long been known as Hometown of Dragons, which have been made into handiworks by local artisans by using materials such as bronze, stone, bamboo, wood, silk, paper, and textiles. These works are great souvenirs for travelers.

Linjiang Folding Fans

Linjiang in Kaixian County has produced folding fans for 160 years. Fine-quality silk and phoenix-tail bamboo are chosen as the raw materials, which are bleached and processed with aroma. With elegant paintings of various patterns, the fans are fragrant, simple, and elegant, making an excellent gift for friends and relatives.

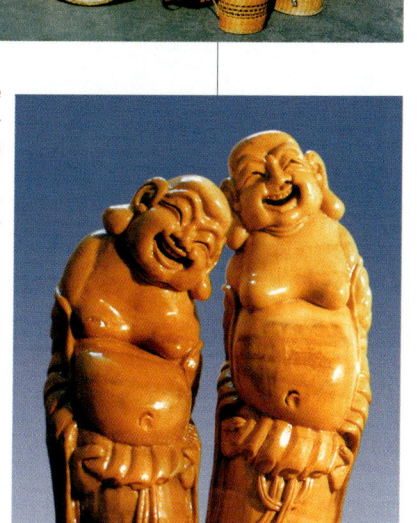

Bamboo carvings.

Rongchang Pottery

Archaeologists prove that Rongchang has a history of 800 years for pottery production. The pottery ware made in Rongchang is practical and elegant, unique in style and look ancient, and they sell well at home and abroad.

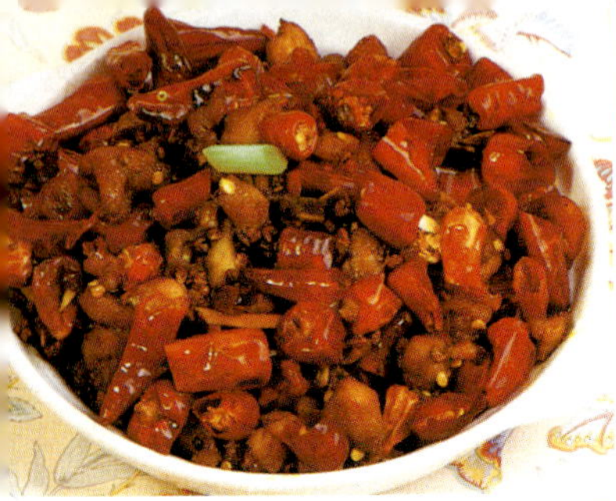
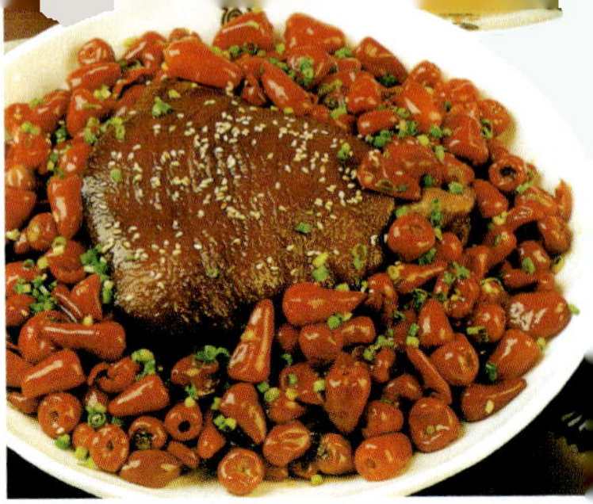
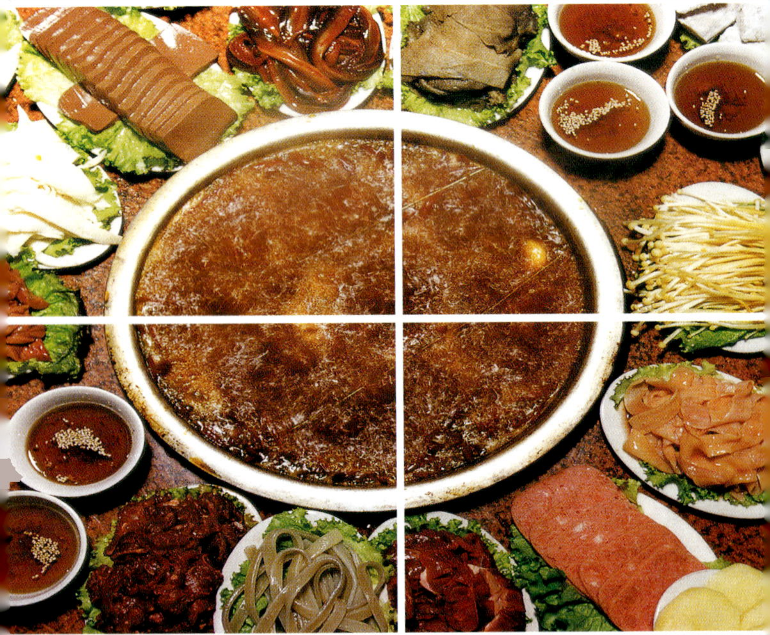
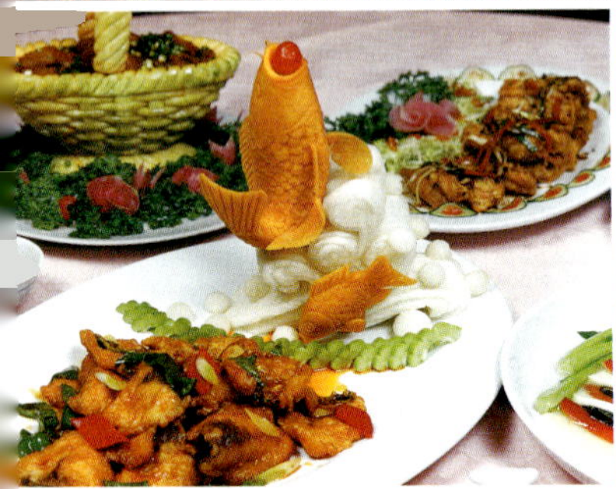
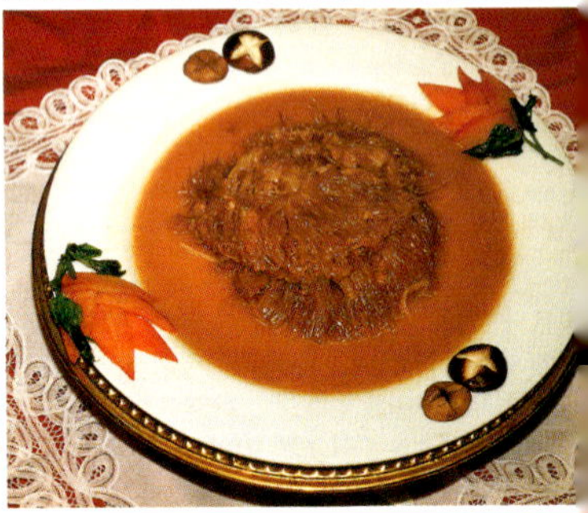
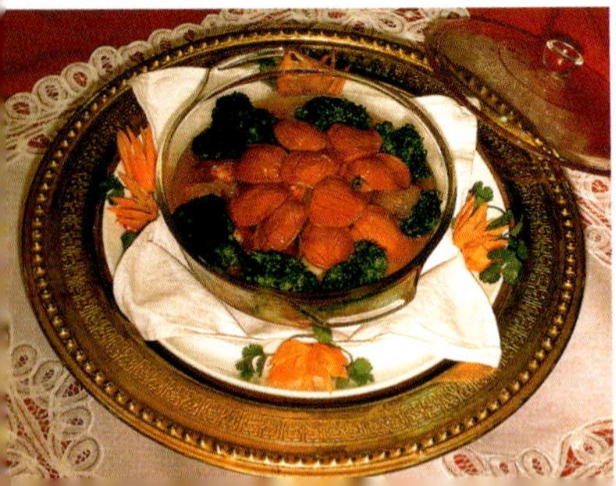
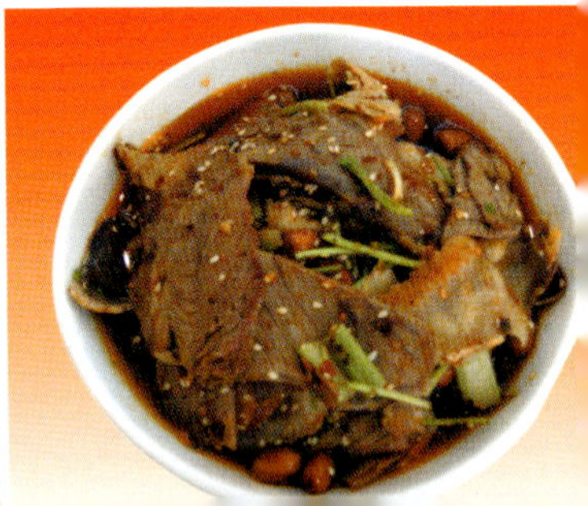

Sichuan Cuisine

Features of Sichuan Dishes

As one of the four most famous cuisine in China, Sichuan cuisine can be divided into four parts, including the local flavors of Chongqing, Chengdu, north Sichuan and south Sichuan. The history of Sichuan cuisine dates back to the Qin and Han Dynasties. In the late third century, when Emperor Qin Shihuang united China, large number of immigrants poured into Sichuan from central China, bringing along with their own cooking styles later accepted by Sichuan local cuisine. This explains the uniqueness of Sichuan dishes, which soon became one of the most popular cuisine in China during the Tang Dynasty. In the Qing Dynasty, chili peppers were introduced to China, adding the flavor to Sichuan cuisine and enriching the menu of Sichuan dishes. When Chongqing became the auxiliary capital during the Anti-Japanese War, many master chefs came to Chongqing, hence upgrading the quality of Sichuan cuisine. There are nearly 40 ways of cooking Sichuan dishes, numbering 3,000 kinds. It has been taken as part of the Sichuan Culture, which can be seen on the menu. High up on the menu are dishes such as Braised Shark's Fin, Steamed Sea Slugs, Steamed Fish Maws, Fried Squid with Litchi, Steamed Jiangtuan Fish, Braised Carpe with Chili Sauce, Sliced Pork cooked on Lotus Leaf, Pig's Leg Cooked with Crystal Sugar, Stir-fried Boiled Pork Slices in Hot Sauce, *Dictyophora Phalloidea* and Pigeon Egg Soup, Crispy Skin Fish, Fish-flavored Shredded Pork, Rice Crust with Sauce of Spiced Sliced Pork, Chongqing Hot Pot, Soft-fried Spareribs, Multi-flavored Chicken Shreds, Cooked Assorted Seeds in Distillers' Grains, and Camphor Branch Smoked Duck.

Styles of Sichuan Dishes

Sichuan cuisine has long focused on the harmony of five flavors. It leads other famous cuisine in China in terms of flavors, 24 in total, that can be divided into three styles: spicy and hot, pungent and delicious, and salty, fresh, sweet and sour.

The spicy and hot style includes the flavors of spicy and hot, chili oil, pepper hot, sour and hot, pepper spicy, simple hot, litchi hot, fish flavor, orange peel flavor, and odd flavor. Fish, orange peel and odd flavors are unique in Sichuan dishes and difficult to prepare. They consists of more than ten ingredients with the tastes of salty, sweet, sour, hot, fresh, and fragrant.

The pungent and delicious style include the flavors of mashed garlic, ginger sauce, mustard, sesame paste, smoke, thick sauce, five spices—prickly ash, star aniseed, cinnamon, clove and fennel—and fermented flavor.

The salty, fresh, sweet and sour style includes salty and fresh, fermented soya beans, salted, tomato sauce, thick sweet, litchi, and sweet and sour.

Nanshan Spring Chicken Street

It is located in Huangjiaoya by Mt. Nanshan Park. Spacious with beautiful surroundings, the street have restaurants of various styles, some of which are located under the trees and among flowers. Over 100 restaurants cater to strongly-flavored local food, most of which are spring chickens. The Nanshan Spring Chicken Festival is held in April here.

Steamed Pork with Longan

Salty and fresh, and thick sweet type. It is a typical dish of local farmers, better known as "covered pork". It is a must dish on a banquet menu or to entertain guests. It is elegant in shape, tender, and fat yet not greasy.

Boiled Beef with Spicy Sauce

Hot and spicy type. It is one of the typical Sichuan dishes, and featured by spicy and hot flavors, fresh and tender.

Many names of the Sichuan dishes are related to the background of Chinese culture. Take a dish called "Liu He Tong Chun"(The whole world is in Spring). Liu He (six dimensions) refers to six directions of east, west, south, north, heaven and earth, which form the universe in Chinese culture. "Liu" and "He" in Sichuan dialect also sounds like "deer" and "crane", which symbolize longevity. Some of the names follow folktales, reminding diners of the past. The names of restaurants are also relevant to traditional Chinese philosophy or customs.

Since China's implementation of the reform and opening-up policies, Chongqing has made great efforts in enriching the menu while maintaining the tradition. Chongqing Hot Pot, for instance, has been served in more forms, such as the Double Flavored, the Four Flavored, and Stewed Fish with Pickled Cabbage, which were popular in the 1980, the series of chicken with chili pepper, the duck and beer, the fish with bean curd jelly, and the hot-spring chicken, which were popular in the 1990s.

The fishing village on the Daxigou River.

Tourism Information

Braised Shark's Fin

Salty and fresh type. Boil shark's fin, chicken, duck, pork, and ham with fresh soup until it's dry. It looks bright, soft, and juicy.

Steamed Sea Slugs

Salty and fresh type. Boil a big sea slug with chicken, ham, dried scallop, winter bamboo shoots, and mushrooms, and steam. It looks bright in color and elegant in shape. It tastes tender and juicy.

Steamed Fish Maws

Salty and fresh type. Boil the fresh yellow croaker with fresh soup and steam it with ham, sliced cucumber, and mushroom. It is elegant in shape and tender in taste. The soup is clear and fresh.

Fresh Stewed Oxtail

Salty and fresh type. It is very strict to select the raw material, the middle section of an oxtail. Soak the oxtail in clear water and boil it in boiling water together with ingredients with low heat. The soup is clear, fresh, and delicious.

Fried Squid with Litchi

Litchi sweet type. Slice fine-quality squid at cross cut and deep fry until they curl. It looks floral, and tastes sweet and chewy. This dish shows the chef's skills in slicing and the control of heat.

Steamed Jiangtuan Fish

Ginger juicy type. Steam Jiangtuan fish, a native product from the Jialing River, in clear soup. Well preserved in shape, it tastes fresh and tender.

Laifeng Fish

The fish from Laifeng Town, Bishan County is boiled. It tastes spicy, hot, fresh, and tender, with a strong local flavor.

Boiled Fish with Pickled Vegetables

A typical dish of local Chongqing, it consists of pickled vegetable and fish with Sichuan-flavored ingredients. It is fresh, somewhat hot, and appetizing.

Braised Carpe with Chili Sauce

Home-made type. Braise a carpe weighing about 600 grams with chili sauce. The fish is well shaped, red in color, and tender and sweet in taste.

Sliced Pork cooked on Lotus Leaf

Salty and fresh type. A seasonal dish, it is a typical dish for the locals to entertain their guests, and tastes fragrant, tender, and fresh.

Pig's Leg Cooked with Crystal Sugar

Salty and sweet type. It is an ordinary dish on the local's table, and looks rich, red, and tender.

Dry Simmered Eel

Hot and spicy type. Dry simmering is a unique way of cooking, and the control of the degree of heat is the key point that only professionals can do. It tastes soft, crispy, hot, and spicy.

Fried Duck

Salty and fresh type. The raw materials include a fat duck, a ham, hydrated dried slices of tender bamboo shoots, mushroom, and fresh soup.

Stir Fried Chicken and Pig's Tripe

Salty and fresh type. Stir frying chicken and pig's tripe, and the key to the success of this dish is the control of the degree of heat.

Stir-fried Boiled Pork Slices in Hot Sauce

Home-made type. A typical Sichuan dish every household can cook but slightly different from one another. The color is nice, and the shape elegant, and it tastes a bit hot.

Dictyophora Phalloidea and Pigeon Egg Soup

Salty and fresh type. Boil *dictyophora phalloidea*, a kind of edible fungus found in bamboo groves, with pigeon eggs. It is nutritious, clear, and refreshing.

Crispy Skin Fish

Sweet and sour type. Deep fry a fresh fish weighing around 800 grams until it's cooked. Pour a sweet and sour source and serve. The skin is crispy, the meat tender.

Fish-flavored Shredded Pork

Fish-flavored type. One of the best on the menu of Sichuan dishes, it is a good example to show the skills of the chef. It looks bright in color, and features a strong flavor of sweet, sour, hot, and spicy of garlic, spring onion, and ginger.

Rice Crust with Sauce of Spiced Sliced Pork

Litchi type. The key to cook this dish properly is the degree of heat. The sliced pork is tender, the rice crust crispy, and it tastes sweet, sour, and fresh.

Chongqing Hot Pot

Spicy and hot mainly, salty, fresh, and hot type. Two kinds of soup, one is clear, another hot, are available. The point to this dish is the meticulously chosen ingredients in the soup, hot, spicy, fresh, and appetizing. It has been popular because it can feed different tastes of diners.

Soft-fried Spareribs

Salty and fresh type. Preserve the selected spareribs with ingredients. Steam and deep fry. It looks beautiful and elegant and tastes crispy and tender.

Multi-flavored Chicken Shreds

Odd taste type. A special on the menu of Sichuan cuisine, it tastes sour, sweet, hot, spicy, salty, and delicious.

Cooked Assorted Seeds in Distillers' Grains

Fry the cakes of fermented rice with sesame, orange cakes, walnut kernel, shelled peanut, candied dates, and sugar, and boil. It is sweet and nutritious, and is a popular food for the local lying-in women.

Camphor Branch Smoked Duck

Smoke fragrance type. It is a typical Sichuan dish and famous for its strict selection of raw materials and complicated ingredients. It used to be a tribute to the royal court. It is salty and appetizing with crispy skin and tender meat.

Stir-fried bean curd in hot sauce.

Shredded Pork with Smashed Garlic

Smashed garlic type. The sauce is red, and the meat is white. It tastes salty, fresh, and a bit hot, with the fragrance of garlic.

Sweet and Sour Spareribs

Sweet and sour type. This dish is the best accompaniment to wine. The proportion of sauce and the control of the degree of heat are the key points to cook the dish.

Five-Spicy Smoked Fish

Five-spicy type. The procedures to cook this dish is complicated and required many ways of cooking, including deep frying, braising, and baking. It is the best dish for wine.

Chicken Shreds

Spicy and hot type. Chicken chest and legs are selected to be boiled in fresh soup. Shred the boiled chicken chest and legs and stir with sauce. While cooking, beat the chicken chest and legs with a stick. Hence the name of the dish.

Glutinous Rice Cake with Sweet Fillings Wrapped in Orange Leaves

Local Snacks

Glutinous Rice Cake with Sweet Fillings Wrapped in Orange Leaves

Steam glutinous rice cakes with sweet fillings of sesame or minced pork wrapped in orange leaves with roaring fire. It tastes fresh, sweet, or salty.

Deep-fried Glutinous Rice Balls

Deep fry glutinous rice balls stuffed with sweet. It is crispy outside and empty inside, and tastes sweet.

Pickled vegetables in jars.

Glutinous Rice Pie

It is made of glutinous rice, sugar, sesame paste, candied osmanthus flower, and bean curd flour. Various in shape, it tastes sweet and chewy.

Deep-fried glutinous rice balls with sweet fillings.

Stuffed Glutinous Rice Dumplings in Soup

Boil dumplings made of glutinous rice flour stuffed with sweet in soup. The dumplings are as crystal as jade pearls, and tastes soft and sweet.

Jiuyuan Steamed Stuffed Buns

Steam the stuffed buns with your favorable salty fillings, such as pork, winter bamboo shoot, dried scallop, and ham, or sweet fillings, such as walnut kernel, candied dates, sliced cucumber with condiments, and dried oranges.

Tourism Information

Iron Cake
Stir rice flour with eggs, sugar, and candied osmanthus flowers. Bake them in a pan till they turn to golden, and serve.

Noodles with Spicy Sauce
A typical local food, the noodles, soft and spicy, is cooked with more than 10 ingredients, especially spicy sauce.

Cold Noodles with Sliced Chicken
Boil thin noodles and cool. Stir with sliced chicken or other ingredients, and serve.

Sichuan Wontons Served in Soup
The filling is meticulously made with minced pork with a certain proportion of water. Boil wontons in the soup and serve.

Guoqiao Wontons
It is famous for its unique way of eating. When it's served, pick one out and dip in spicy sauce in a small plate.

Fried Dumplings with Chicken Sauce
Stuff the wraps with minced pork of necessary ingredients and chicken sauce and bake in the pan with a cover.

Jellied Bean Curd with Sliced Chicken
It is made of grinned bean curd and served together with cooked chicken slices and your favorite ingredients, spicy and hot, maybe.

Puffed Rice with Sweet Water
Boil the puffed rice in sweet water. It used to be sold by hawkers on the street.

Boiled glutinous rice balls.

Noodles with spicy sauce.

Sichuan wontons in soup.

Bean curd jelly with chicken shreds.

Tourist Accommodation

The Japanese Restaurant of Marriott Hotel.

Marriott Hotel.

As one of China's popular tourist cities, Chongqing has sufficient modern tourist service facilities, that can meet the needs of tourists at all levels with start-rated hotels, hotels designated by tourism administrations, ordinary hotels, and guest houses. There are 42 foreign-oriented hotels above three stars, including Marriott, Wanyoukangnian, Holiday Inn Yangtze, Renmin Hotel, and Chongqing Hotel, 59 above one-star hotels and hotels designated by tourism administrations, and thousands of hotels and guest houses.

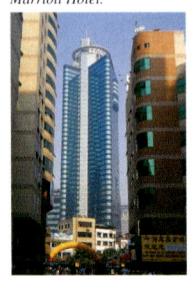

Marriott Hotel ★★★★

Located at 77 Qingnian Road, Yuzhong District, Marriott has presidential suites, administration suites and guestrooms, and deluxe guestrooms and suites. There are facilities, including Chinese, Japanese, and Western restaurants, bar, health center, sauna, hydraulic massage pools, indoor swimming pool, and health club with facilities for table tennis, billards, and chess.

Harbour Plaza Hotel ★★★★★

Located at Wuyi Road in the Yuzhong District, adjacent to the Metropolis Square, Harbour Plaza has service facilities, such as café, the Yangtze Wine Corridor, the Chinese restaurant, a large gymnasium, an indoor swimming pool, a bar, and a tennis court. There is also a mall, with bowling alleys, a skating rink, a movie theater, and office buildings.

Harbour Plaza Hotel.

Hilton Hotel ★★★★★

Located in the Yuzhong District, where the Yangtze and Jialing Rivers meet, Hilton Hotel is an ideal choice for business travel and amusement. It is only four kilometers from the Monument to Liberation, the busiest commercial center in the city, and an 35-minute drive from the airport. There are 441 guestrooms and suites and 42 rooms for the disabled. All rooms are equipped with facilities for the Internet access. There are swimming pool, gym, and beauty saloon. The

The lounge of Hilton Hotel.

West Asia Hotel ★★★★

Located in the Chongqing Hi-Tech Development District, the West Asia has facilities, including Chinese and Western restaurants, high-class guestrooms, a bar, a beauty saloon, a sauna, a nightclub, a karaoke lounge, a health club, a chess room, an electric games center, a jazz bar, meeting rooms, and a business center.

Wanyou Kangnian Hotel.

Wanyou Kangnian Hotel ★★★★

Under the administration of the Hong Kong Kangnian Hotel Management Co., the Hotel building is 32 storied, towering at 77 Changjiang Erlu in Daping. It has Chinese and Western restaurants, three bars of different styles, meeting rooms, and facilities for recreation and health. It has presidential suites, deluxe apartments, deluxe guestrooms, high-class guestrooms, and standard guestrooms, all equipped with the Internet access, fax, DDD/IDD telephone, voice mail system, safe, and international cable TV.

Holiday Inn Yangtze.

Holiday Inn Yangtze ★★★★

Located in the Nanping Economic & Technological Development District, Holiday Inn Yangtze has standard rooms, deluxe rooms, apartments, and presidential suites equipped with DDD/IDD telephone, voice mail system, and international cable TV. Guests can enjoy different styles of cuisine from most parts of the world, including Sichuan and Cantonese dishes, and Chongqing snacks. The hotel also has a gym, a billiard room, a sauna, a tennis court, a golf course, and an outdoor swimming pool.

2,300-square-meter indoor facilities is under the management of the professional company in accordance with international standard.

Chongqing Guest House ★★★★

Chongqing Guest House, one of China's Top Star-Rated Hotels, is located in the business center, with traditional Chinese garden-style architectures and convenient transportation and telecommunication. It has 267 guestrooms, the Dragon-Phoenix Chinese Restaurant, the Yalan Western Restaurant, the Sunshine Seafood, the Flavored Hot Pot, and the Apollo Nightclub. Guests can enjoy typical Sichuan and Cantonese food, Chongqing Hot Pot, and local snacks; ease away their spare time in the Amusement Center, the Nightclub, and the Ballroom enjoying Chinese and foreign performances; or go shopping in the Sunshine Mall.

The lounge of Chongqing Guest House.

World Traders Hotel ★★★★

Located in the busy commercial area with convenient transportation, the World Traders Hotel is a four-star hotel of international standard especially for business travelers. There are elegant, comfortable guestrooms, a well-facilitated, multi-function banquet hall, the grand Seafood, the secluded Business Teahouse, the foreign-styled Swan Café, and the Dream-in-the-Cloud Club, where people can be totally relaxed.

World Traders Hotel.

Fog City Hotel ★★★★

fog City Hotel is located in the Yuzhong District, with the Jialing River in the north, Mt. Pipa Park in the south, and and adjacent to the famous tourist attraction, Zhou's Mansion. The hotel provides 350 standard rooms, deluxe suites, and presidential suites. The environment is quiet, and the service excellent. There are facilities, including the Sauna, the Swimming Pool, and the Bowling Alley.

Fog City Hotel.

Renmin Hotel ★★★

Located on Renmin Road in central Chongqing, and part of the People's Great Hall, the Hotel has a splendid, grandeur palace of traditional Chinese style, with elegant interior facilities, and a colorful modern square, which makes the hotel one of the symbolically-structured hotels in China. There are 214 rooms and restaurants in Sichuan, Chongqing, and Cantonese styles. Guests can enjoy their spare time in the Palace Nightclub, the Electric-Games House, the Gym, the Beauty Saloon, and the Bar.

The lounge of Renmin Hotel.

Guangchang Hotel ★★★

The Hotel is situated on Xuetianwan Zhengjie, where the office building of the Municipal Government of Chongqing is located. It is one of the symbolic structures in the city, and has convenient transportation. It provides comfortable, well-equipped guestrooms and services for food, tourist guide, telecommunication, and meetings.

Chongqing Grand Hotel.

Chongqing Grand Hotel ★★★

The hotel is located in the Shapingba District, near Chongqing University and Chongqing Architecture University. The hotel has 240 guestrooms, Sichuan Restaurant, Cantonese Restaurant, Banquet Hall, Western Restaurant, Bar, Café, Gymnasium, Nightclub, Shopping Center, Multi-function Hall, and meeting rooms. There are other services, such as medical, car rent, ticket reservation, tourist guide, foreign currency exchange. The pleasant environment and convenient transportation makes the hotel a perfect choice for tourists and business travelers.

Chung King Hotel ★★★

Located near Chaotian Gate at the junction of the Yangtze and Jialing Rivers, Chung King Hotel is the first three-star hotel in Chongqing. The hotel is a tall European-style building built in the 1940s, with comfortable, safe and well-equipped rooms, grand Chinese and Western restaurants, café, and bar. Also available are such service facilities as a beauty saloon, a clinic, a recreation center, and the sauna.

Chung King Hotel.

Milky Way hotel ★★★

The Milky Way Hotel is located at the hub of the business center by the Monument to Liberation, thus enjoying convenient transportation. Although in business center, it is quiet inside. Guests can enjoy Chinese and Western food as well as local snacks in the hotel, and walk around the City of Mountains, admire the night view of Chongqing, and feel the pulse of the real life.

The Japanese Restaurant of the Milky Way Hotel.

Jianshe Hotel ★★★

Jianshe Hotel.

Jianshe Hotel is located at the starting point of the Chengdu-Chongqing Expressway. The hotel has quiet and refreshing environment, convenient transportation, and excellent services for business talks, meetings, and holiday making.

Southwest Hotel ★★★

The Southwest Hotel is the major part of the Southwest Economic Cooperation Complex in the Nanping Economic and Technological Development District. It has 265 guestrooms, 17 meeting rooms, banquet halls, and KTV rooms. The restaurant is large enough to accommodate 600 people at one time. Other services include taxi, ticket reservation, entertainment, gym, and medical treatment. Featuring a strong cultural flavor of Southwest China, the hotel is the best choice for business travelers and holiday makers.

Little Swan Hotel ★★★

The Little Swan Hotel is located in the Jiangbei Economic Development District on the northern bank of the Jialing River, a 20-minute drive from the airport, 12-minute drive to the harbor, and 8-minute drive to the railway station. The hotel has state-of-the-art facilities, pleasant environment, and first-class service.

Little Swan Hotel.

Tourism Information

Dazu Hotel ★★★

Dazu Hotel, the first three-star hotel of international standard, is located at in central Dazu County, half an hour's walk to the Stone Carvings scenic area in Mt. Beishan. Its complete facilities, pleasant interior environment, and perfect service make it an ideal place for tourists and business travelers.

Dazu Hotel.

Yuzhou Hotel ★★★

Located in the Chongqing High-Tech Development District in the western suburbs, Yuzhou Hotel is a garden-like complex with lawns, zig-zagging corridors, and a beautiful lake. Available are deferent classes of rooms, restaurants, conference halls, swimming pool, billiard room, tennis court, meeting all need of business travelers, tourists, and conference participants.

The restaurant of the Yutong Hotel.

Yutong Hotel ★★★

Located beside the Hongqihegou Flyover in the Yubei District, Yutong Hotel is a garden-like, modern hotel with unique architectural style, a beautiful environment, and excellent service. It has 130 well-decorated standard rooms, deluxe suites, a ballroom, a billiard room, an amusement center, a swimming pool, a sauna, a beauty saloon, and meeting rooms for all kinds of gatherings.

Sunshine Hot Spring Holiday Village ★★★

The Sunshine Hot Spring Holiday Village is located in South Hot Spring scenic area at the foot of mountains and by the riverside of Huaxi. The European-style buildings are in the shade of lush trees and waterfalls. An international-standard three-star hotel, this complex is the right choice for business traveling and holiday making, with food, accommodation, recreation, sightseeing, and shopping. It has villas, deluxe rooms, standard rooms, meeting rooms, Chinese and Western restaurants, Piano Bar, Roof Garden Teahouse, and Picnic BBQ, in addition to recreational center, gym, business center, and shopping arcade. It takes only half an hour's drive from the city proper.

The Sunshine Hot Spring Holiday Village.

Star-Rated Hotels in Chongqing

Name	Star	Tel (023)	Fax (023)	Address	Postal code
Marriott Hotel	☆☆☆☆☆	6388 8888	6388 8777	77 Qingnian Rd., Yuzhong Dist.	400010
Harbour Plaza Hotel	☆☆☆☆☆	6370 0888	6370 0778	Wuyi Rd., Yuzhong Dist.	400010
Hilton Hotel	☆☆☆☆☆	8903 9999	8903 8700	139 Zhongshan Sanlu, Yuzhong Dist.	400010
Holiday Inn Yangtze	☆☆☆☆	6280 8888	6280 0884	15 North Nanping Rd., Nan'an Dist.	400060
Chongqing Guest House	☆☆☆☆	6384 5888	6383 0643	235 Minsheng Rd.	400010
Wanyou Kangnian Hotel	☆☆☆☆	6871 8888	6871 3333	77 Changjiang Erlu, Yuzhong Dist.	400042
West Asia Hotel	☆☆☆☆	6860 0999	6860 0084	33 Yuzhou Rd., Shiqiaopu	400039
Kinglead Hotel	☆☆☆☆	6862 6666	6862 2222	9 Keyuan Erlu, Shiqiaopu	400039
Liyuan Hotel	☆☆☆☆	6531 6666	6531 9999	15 Tianchen Rd., Shapingba Dist.	400030
Holtak Hotel	☆☆☆☆	6283 8888	6280 5747	318 South Nanping Rd.	400060
World Traders Hotel	☆☆☆☆	6378 1111	6378 1400	118 Zourong Rd., Yuzhong Dist.	400010
Huabang Hotel	☆☆☆☆	7773 7777	7773 7333	Mt. Fairy Maiden, Wulong County	408500
Jinguan Grand Hotel	☆☆☆☆	7931 0999	7931 0988	Santaishan Park, Qianjiang Dist.	409000
Taiji Grand Hotel	☆☆☆☆	7288 8888	7222 4555	South Tiyu Rd., Fuling Dist.	408000
Donghe Garden Hotel	☆☆☆☆	6753 1888	6753 1910	99 Honghuang Rd., Yuzhong Dist.	401147
Fog City Hotel	☆☆☆☆	6385 1788	6385 0762	24 Shangzengjiayan, Yuzhong Dist.	400015
Oriental Garden Hotel	☆☆☆☆	6389 2666	6385 3332	55 Tianwan Zhengjie, Yuzhong Dist.	400015
Huangjia Hotel	☆☆☆☆	6352 8888	6352 9999	85 Zhongshan Yilu, Yuzhong Dist.	400013
Chung King Hotel	☆☆☆	6383 8888	6384 3085	41 Xinhua Rd., Yuzhong Dist.	400010
Renmin Hotel	☆☆☆	6385 6888	6385 2076	173 Renmin Rd.,	400015
Chongqing Grand Hotel	☆☆☆	6533 9888	6531 3293	84 Xiaolongkan Xinjie, Shapingba Dist.	400030
Jianshe Hotel	☆☆☆	6881 8888	6881 5132	8-88 Xiejiawan Zhengjie, Jiulongpo Dist.	400050
Dazu Hotel	☆☆☆	4372 1888	4372 2827	47 Gongnong St., Dazu County	402360
Milky Way Hotel	☆☆☆	6380 8585	6381 2080	49 Datong Rd., Yuzhong Dist.	400010
Southwest Hotel	☆☆☆	6280 2901	6280 0911	5 North Nanping Rd., Nan'an Dist.	400060
Little Swan Hotel	☆☆☆	6786 8888	6770 1518	78 North Jianxin Rd., Jiangbei Dist.	400020
Sunshine Hot Spring Holiday Village	☆☆☆	6284 8199	6284 9048	South Hot Spring	400056
Hongdu Hotel	☆☆☆	6387 0566	6385 9530	2 Jialingqiao Xicun, Yuzhong Dist.	400015
Chaotianmen Hotel	☆☆☆	6310 1888	6371 3035	18 Xinyi St., Yuzhong Dist.	400011
Hongsheng Holiday Resort	☆☆☆	7224 4666	7223 7959	100 Wangzhou Rd., Fuling Dist	400032
Jialing Hotel	☆☆☆	6519 2518	6519 4151	Zhanjiaxi, Shuangbei, Shapingba Dist.	400032
Yutong Hotel	☆☆☆	6752 5226	6752 3522	18 Hongjin Blv., Hongqihegou, Yubei Dist.	400020
Jialehui Grand Hotel	☆☆☆	7225 8888	7226 1339	53 Middle Xinghua Rd., Fuling Dist.	408000
Yudu Grand Hotel	☆☆☆	6382 8888	6381 8168	168 Bayi Rd., Yuzhong Dist.	400010
Yangtze Island Hotel	☆☆☆	6371 8888	6373 9886	-1 82 Zourong Rd., Yuzhong Dist.	400010

Star-Rated Hotels in Chongqing

Name	Star	Tel (023)	Fax (023)	Address	Postal code
Jiangzhou Hotel	☆☆☆	4752 6888	4752 6888	12 Middle Binjiang Rd., Jiangjin	402260
Zhongtian Hotel	☆☆☆	6373 9898	6371 3827	18 Qingnian Rd., Yuzhong Dist.	400010
Sote Hotel	☆☆☆	5896 0978	5896 0444	Guanyinyan, Wanzhou Dist.	404005
Fuling Hotel	☆☆☆	7225 9999	7224 7777	Middle Xinghua Rd., Fuling Dist.	400080
Guangchang Hotel	☆☆☆	6389 6868	6389 6260	2 Xuetianwan Zhengjie, Yuzhong Dist.	400015
Tongnan Hotel	☆☆☆	4455 0988	4456 0788	38 Shiyuan St., Tongnan County	402660
Egret Mansion	☆☆☆	6574 0466	6574 0456	Sanduoqiao Village, Baishiyi Town	401329
South Garden Hotel	☆☆☆	6863 4567	6860 8199	198 Keyuan Silu, South Garden	400039
Dongfang Hotel	☆☆☆	6258 9888	6258 0999	Huaxi Town, Banan Dist.	400054
Tongliang Hotel	☆☆☆	4569 0888	4569 0999	1 Yingbin Blv., Tongliang County	402560
Millennium Hotel	☆☆☆	5810 4999	5810 4891	136 Taibai Rd., Wanzhou	404000
Yangtze Grand Hotel	☆☆☆	5814 0088	5813 6600	218 Taibai Rd., Wanzhou	404000
Peace Hotel	☆☆☆	6732 0999	6732 0997	42 Shiyang Rd., Chongqing Hi-Tech District	400039
Hongdu Grand Hotel	☆☆☆	5768 9999	5703 9888	Middle Jixian Rd., Wushan County	404700
Fragrant Hill Hotel	☆☆☆	6290 6888	6280 5846	66 Zhengjie St., Nanping Dist.	400060
Peach City Hotel	☆☆☆	6878 1818	6842 4244	21 Xijiao Rd., Yangjiaping	400050
Jinjiang Hotel	☆☆☆	6840 3888	6878 3699	24 Xijiao Rd., Yangjiaping, Jiulong Dist.	400050
Great Wall Hotel	☆☆☆	5810 0788	5812 2388	74 West St., Yongchuan City	402160
Yongchuan Hotel	☆☆☆	4986 9999	4986 6888	22 Xidajie., Yongchuan	402160
Hot Spring Holiday Village	☆☆☆	6728 8999	6728 8099	Tongling Scenic Area, Yubei Dist.	401124
Chongbai Hotel	☆☆☆	6353 6555	6353 6709	86 Zhongshan Sanlu, Yuzhong Dist.	400015
Golden Swallow Hotel	☆☆☆	6363 5333	6386 6461	188 Nanqu Rd., Yuzhong Dist.	400014
Swan Lake Hotel	☆☆☆	5226 8333	5226 8168	Jingmao Rd., Hanxin Town, Kaixian County	405400
Three Gorges Wind Hotel	☆☆☆	5424 8888	5424 8888	11 Guoyuan Rd., Zhongxian County	404300
Hongsheng Hotel	☆☆☆	6290 9888	6282 7515	1 Nanxing Rd., Nanping	400060
Jinhui Hotel	☆☆☆	5768 0466	5768 1733	Guangdong Rd., Wushan County	404700
Rhinoceros Hotel	☆☆☆	6782 5888	6782 5888	190 Shengli Rd., Yubei Dist.	401120
Xinhua Hotel	☆☆☆	6780 1376	6780 5833	138 Shuanglong Blv., Yubei Dist.	401120
Bailiwei Hotel	☆☆☆	4862 1666	4861 8520	88 Ansha Rd., Qijiang Development Dist.	401420
Yangxin Hotel	☆☆☆	6908 5858	6908 5599	18 Qianjin Rd., Yangjiaping	400050
Mt. Jinfeng Hotel	☆☆☆	4025 8888	4025 6666	191 Changshou Rd., Changshou County	401220
Zhongzhou Hotel	☆☆☆	5424 4949	5424 4848	127 Pinglu Rd., Zhongzhou Town	404300
New Century Creation Hotel	☆☆☆	6907 8888	6907 9999	1-1 Xinpaifang Rd., Yubei Dist.	401120

Room Reservation at Hotels

In order to secure a pleasant, safe tour, you need to choose and reserve an ideal hotel. You can book through telephone and letter (or fax, telex) as followed:

1. Learn about the basic facts of the hotel, including the class of the rooms, the price, its location, and service facilities.

2. Inform the hotel's Reservation Department or Front Desk about your time of arrival, the type and number of rooms, the duration of your stay, your name, and your contact numbers. Tell them other requirements if you have any, such as receiving at the airport, harbor or railway station, and other services.

3. Confirm your reservation three days prior to your arrival. Please take notes of the time of your calling and the name of the person you are talking to for future check, just in case. Ask for a letter of confirmation from the hotel if possible so that your room can be reserved until 18:00 of your arrival.

4. You'd better remit to the hotel the prepayment of the room for the first day to make sure that the room is reserved even though you cannot make it as scheduled.

FAQ for Traveling in Chongqing

Best Season for Traveling in Chongqing

Chongqing has a complicated geological condition and rich tourism resources. Its tourist attractions are widely scattered with different temperatures. That explains why the metropolis is attractive for tourists all year round. However, the best season for traveling is between March to June, and September and November. Winter is mild, some 6°C, most of the time, with no snow or ice.

How to apply in a travel agency?

Tourists can apply in the local travel agencies, tell them your plan, signing an agreement, and pay as required. All your tour will be taken care of by the travel agency according to the agreement.

What currency and credit cards can be used in Chongqing?

At present, traveler's checks are not widely used in China. Most tourists have to bring cash and credit cards. Overseas tourists can exchange their own currencies, including US Dollars, Euro, Pound Sterling, Yen, Swiss Franc, Australian Dollar, Canadian Dollar, Singapore Dollar, Macao *Pataca*, Malaysia Ringgit, Philippine Peso, Thailand Baht, Austrian Shilling, and New Zealand Dollar, into RMB in the Bank of China in Chongqing and other currency exchange offices in large shopping centers and hotels.

Three-star and above hotels can accept more than ten credit cards, including Dinner Club, American Express, Visa, JCB, Great Wall, Peony, Pacific, and Dragon.

Immigration Check

Before leaving China for trips in other countries, you have to get a visa from the relevant embassies, consulates, and offices with authorities to issue a visa, in China, unless with agreement on mutual exemption of visas.

The immigration officers have to check the entry-departure card and your passport on the arrival and departure, stamp on your passport, and let go.

Tourists have to leave before the valid date of the visa indicated on the passport.

The Chinese government adopts measures for tourists from the countries that have special policies on the entry and departure of Chinese citizens on the reciprocity basis.

Transportation Security Check

According to the regulations made by the Chinese government, lethal weapons, ammunition, flammable material, corrosive material, poisonous material, and radioactive material are restricted on board for any flight, vessel, train, and bus by any one. All tourists must be through the security check prior to boarding. Any one who refuses it will bear the legal responsibility.

Customs

At the customs, there are "Red Channel" and "Green Channel". "Red channel" is for those who have dutiable luggage or staff for customs declaration. "Green Channel" is for other tourists.

Before clear customs, tourists have to fill in a form, "Luggage Customs Declaration". Those from Hong Kong and Macao have to fill in a Return ID, and declare their luggage and belongings. All luggage have to be checked by the customs, and they are not allowed to be taken unless permitted. Keep the declaration form properly because it will be useful on your entry and departure.

Travel Agencies

A travel Agency is a service that makes arrangement for transportation, accommodation, tour, food, amusement, shopping, and tourist guide for the tourists. In China, there are two categories, international and domestic. The international travel agencies provide travel services for foreign visitors, overseas Chinese, and tourists from Hong Kong, Macao, and Taiwan, who travel on China's mainland, and Chinese citizens who want to travel abroad as well as on China's mainland. The domestic travel agencies provide travel services only for Chinese citizens who want to travel

What shall I do if I loose my passport or other IDs?

Report to the local public security bureau as soon as you find yourself in such a trouble. Apply for the permit of departure and paper for the evidence of the loss at a local Foreigner's Administration of Entry and Departure with any proves of your ID, the proves of your loss by your travel agency, and your photos. You can apply for a new passport from your embassy in China with relevant papers.

If you want to prolong tourist visa, apply to the immigration office of the Public Security Bureau with relevant papers.

How shall I communicate if I don't know the language?

If you encounter any language difficulty in transportation, accommodation, and shopping, you can find relevant information in your own language. You can also consult your tourist guide or hotel staff, who can help you out in any languages.

How to find the way when visiting friends in Chongqing?

It happens that you lose your way when you look around in Chongqing for sightseeing or visiting friends. You can tell your tourist guide or the hotel staff your friend's detailed information, including address and the name of his unit, and they will surely help you. If you know the accurate address of your friend, you can take a taxi, and the driver will take you to the place.

Helping friends from afar.

Tourist Health

Some of the tourists do not feel well due to the change of geographic environment and the habits of life. Tourists are advised to keep a good heart and try to live a regular life. It is necessary to bring some medicine for carsickness, cold, diarrhea, pain relieve, paste for wounds, balm for mosquito bites, throat lozenge, and 10 drops, a popular liquid medicine for summer ailments, but don't take any medication if unnecessary.

Traveling, especially a long journey, is tough. Go to your doctor and ask for his advice before you start the journey. We strongly suggest to postpone or cancel your trip if you belong to any of the following cases:

1. Victims of serious heart and cerebral diseases;

2. Patients during the period of infection, treatment, and inflammation;

3. Recovering period after an operation;

4. Sufferer of seasonal asthma;

5. Victims of uncontrollable epilepsy and mental diseases.

on China's mainland.

Tourism has become a pillar industry in China thanks to the rapid development over the last few years. Today, there are 20 international travel agencies and 185 domestic travel agencies in Chongqing, ready to serve friends from all parts of the world.

Tourism Information

Major International Travel Services

Name	Address	Postal Code	Telephone	Fax
Overseas Tourism (Travel Service) Group Ltd.	120 Yazheng St., Zilan, Yuzhong Dist.	400015	63718258	63850095
Merchants Int'l Travel Service Ltd.	99 Zhongshan Erlu, Yuzhong Dist.	400014	63516391	63516500
Chongqing Branch, China Travel Service Co., Ltd.	39 Wusi Rd., Yuzhong District	400010	63782666	63803333
Xinya Int'l Travel Service Co., Ltd.	Zourong Plaza, Jiefangbei, Yuzhong Dist.	400010	69037587	69037588
New Century Int'l Travel Service Co., Ltd.	41-42 Datong St., Yuzhong Dist.	400011	63775942	63810992
Chongqing Branch, China Int'l Travel Service Co., Ltd.	114 Yazheng St., Zilan, Yuzhong Dist.	400015	63894005	63850196
Yangtze River Cruise Int'l Travel Service	99 Zhongshan Erlu, Yuzhong Dist.	400014	63522955	63505789
Yangtze River Int'l Travel Service	72 Jixian St., Wuxi Town	404700	57822269	57282169
Huifeng Int'l Travel Service Co., Ltd.	19 Shangye St., Mingshan Town, Fengdu County	408200	70623707	70322594
Chongqing Branch, China Youth Travel Service Co., Ltd.	109 Zourong Rd., Yuzhong Dist.	400010	63709619	63905408
Chongqing Everbright Int'l Travel Service Co., Ltd.	76 North Jianxin Rd., Jiangbei Dist.	400020	67736952	67727276
Swan Int'l Travel Co.	168 Zhongshan Sanlu, Yuzhong Dist.	400013	63631561	63613174
Wanyou Int'l Travel Service	77 Changjiang Erlu, Yuzhong Dist.	400042	78770782	68770721

Top Five International Travel Services & Top Ten Domestic Travel Services in 2000

Name	Address	Postal Code	Telephone	Fax
Overseas Tourism (Travel Service) Group Ltd.	120 Yazheng St., Zilan, Yuzhong Dist.	400015	63718258	63850095
New Century Int'l Travel Service Co., Ltd.	41-42 Datong St., Yuzhong Dist.	400011	63775942	63810992
Merchants Int'l Travel Service Ltd.	99 Zhongshan Erlu, Yuzhong Dist.	400014	63516391	63516500
Xinya Int'l Travel Service Co., Ltd.	Zourong Plaza, Jiefangbei, Yuzhong Dist.	400010	69037587	69037588
Yangtze River Cruise Int'l Travel Service	99 Zhongshan Erlu, Yuzhong Dist.	400014	63522955	63505789
Spring & Autumn Travel Service	268 Minsheng Rd., Yuzhong Dist.	400010	63834231	63727393
Yangtze River Sightseeing Int'l Travel Service Co., Ltd.	51 Xinhua Rd., Yuzhong Dist.	400011	63814476	63844984
Taixiang Travel Service	16-1 Zhongshan Erlu, Yuzhong Dist.	400014	63853389	63868909
Jiangzhou Travel Co., Ltd.	219 West Jiefang Rd., Yuzhong Dist.	400012	63713064	63822890
Yushen Travel Service	15 Shunchenglou, Linjiangmen, Yuzhong Dist.	400010	63717225	63717226
Rail Travel Service	5 Zhongshan Zhilu, Yuzhong Dist.	400014	61644533	63531025
Hengda Travel Co.	Xijiao Sancun, Jiulongpo Dist.	400050	68782205	68427931
Changhang Jiangshan Travel Service	4 Shaanxi Rd., Yuzhong Dist.	400011	63718084	63773017
Comfort Broadcast & TV Travel Service	177 Zhongshan Sanlu, Yuzhong Dist.	400015	63600191	63602519
Tianhai Travel Service	5 Xinhua Rd., Yuzhong Dist.	400011	63831159	63714844

Special Telephone Numbers   Area code: 023

Police	110	Tourist Special Bus	6373 5304
Fire	119	Traffic accident	6881 0501
Weather	121	Taxi complaint	6787 1530
First aid	120	Taxi police	6880 8074
First-aid medicine	6384 1026	Consumer complaint	6371 0315
Blood station	6385 0901	Consumer report	12315
CAAC information	6715 2335	Passenger complaint	6386 4421
Air ticket reservation	6386 2970	Industrial & Commercial Bureau complaint	6373 3074
Railway station	6386 2607		
Harbor passenger transport	6384 1342	Legal supervision complaint	6371 2478
Long-distance bus station	6387 3196	Entry & departure information	6375 9470

Tourist Complaint Area code: 023

Chongqing	6370 5525 or 6389 0134	Bishan County	4142 7414
Yuzhong Dist.	6373 5164	Rongchang County	4673 3551
Jiangbei Dist.	6787 0354	Changshou Conty	4024 5793
Nan'an Dist.	6292 3724	Dianjiang County	7452 7733
Shapingba Dist.	6531 2971	Fengdu County	7060 5698
Jiulongpo Dist.	6842 3023	Wulong County	7772 1248
Banan District	6622 8249	Liangping County	6322 2383 Ext. 8888
Beibei Dist.	6821 6220	Zhongxian County	5423 2539
Yubei Dist.	6780 0765	Chengkou County	5922 3366
Shuangqiao Dist.	4333 2779	Yunyang County	5556 2128
Wansheng Dist.	4827 2104	Kaixian County	5222 3059
Fuling Dist.	7222 4375	Wuxi County	5152 2062
Wanzhou Dist.	5824 4509	Fengjie County	5651 2333
Hechuan City	4284 2430	Wushan County	5722 1844
Yongchuan City	4988 1048	Qianjiang County	7923 7986
Jiangjin City	4752 2878	Shizhu County	7333 7520
Nanchuan City	7142 2953	Youyang County	7555 6441
Tongnan County	4456 0793	Pengshui County	7884 3685
Dazu County	4372 7651	Xiushan County	7666 2667
Tongliang County	4563 5787	Dadukou Dist.	6883 0887

Foreign Government Offices

Canadian Consulate	Tel: (023) 6373 8007
Add.: Rm 1705 Metropolitan Mansion, Wuyi Rd., Yuzhong Dist.	Postal code: 400011
Chongqing Office, Japanese Embassy	Tel: (023) 6373 3585
Add.: 14th Fl., Yangguang Mansion, Yuzhong Dist.	Postal code: 400011
British Consulate	Tel: (023) 6381 0321
Add.: Rm. 2802 Metropolitan Mansion, Wuyi Rd., Yuzhong Dist.	Postal code: 400011